高职 PGT
英语口语教程

- 主　编　刘升民　刘小芹
- 参　编　付小云　张敬衡　柳　玲　薛　蕾
　　　　　喻互助　李　京　戴　遂　邹杏梓
　　　　　李　璐　王　苗　刘　艺
- 主　审　Peter Robert Howard　张　欣
- 参　审　舒秀娟　连园园　闻书玲

华中科技大学出版社
http://www.hustp.com
中国·武汉

内 容 提 要

本书以贴合实际生活的各个场景作为背景,编写设计了一系列简单实用的对话,满足学生日常生活所需。设置的对话背景主要有校园生活、购物、公共交通、银行业务、旅游、餐饮、娱乐文化、求职面试、公共安全等。在对话学习完毕之后,还有12套相关练习,学生可以根据其中设定的要求和背景进行表演练习。另外,为了方便读者学习,本书还有配套的词汇表。本书适合于职业院校学生作为教材,也可供涉外工作者和国际商旅人士学习参考。

图书在版编目(CIP)数据

高职 PGT 英语口语教程/刘升民,刘小芹主编.—武汉:华中科技大学出版社,2020.9(2022.9 重印)
ISBN 978-7-5680-6585-6

Ⅰ.①高… Ⅱ.①刘… ②刘… Ⅲ.①英语-口语-高等职业教育-教材 Ⅳ.①H319.32

中国版本图书馆 CIP 数据核字(2020)第 169637 号

高职 PGT 英语口语教程　　　　　　　　　　　　　　　刘升民　刘小芹　主编
Gaozhi PGT Yingyu Kouyu Jiaocheng

策划编辑：陈培斌　兰　刚
责任编辑：李文星
封面设计：刘　婷
责任校对：李　琴
责任监印：周治超

出版发行：华中科技大学出版社(中国·武汉)　　　电话：(027)81321913
　　　　　武汉市东湖新技术开发区华工科技园　　　邮编：430223
录　　排：华中科技大学惠友文印中心
印　　刷：武汉科源印刷设计有限公司
开　　本：787mm×1092mm　1/16
印　　张：7.5　插页:1
字　　数：206 千字
版　　次：2022 年 9 月第 1 版第 3 次印刷
定　　价：28.00 元

本书若有印装质量问题,请向出版社营销中心调换
全国免费服务热线：400-6679-118　　竭诚为您服务
版权所有　侵权必究

前　言

　　随着时代的发展,对外贸易、交流的频繁,口语能力的地位日益提升。作为外语外事职业院校,武汉外语外事职业学院认为培养各专业学生的外语口语表达能力至关重要,它关系到将来的实际应用。学院坚持以"突出涉外特色、面向外向型企业、培养外语特长的应用型人才"为办学宗旨,以"外语＋技能"为人才培养特色,积极推进教育教学和人才培养模式改革,培养适应社会需求、特色鲜明、就业前景好、懂专业、会外语的优秀职业技能人才。为激发全体学生外语学习兴趣,提高外语口语表达能力,实现各专业学生的外语综合应用能力,学院以英语先行,全面推行日语、韩语、法语、西班牙语等多语种"369PGT"外语学习模式,并实施应用外国语综合能力测试,鼓励学生获得学院颁发的应用外国语能力水平测试(证书),以提高学生的外语应用能力。

　　"369PGT"学习模式中,PGT分别代表可采取partner(搭档)、group(小组)、team(团队)进行学习的模式,以课外自主学习为主,课内学习为辅,课内学习与课外学习相结合的学习模式。"369PGT"学习模式即在三个学年中,一年掌握300句,两年掌握600句,三年掌握900句;也可理解为专业英语300句,公共英语600句,共掌握900句;还可理解为应用外国语能力等级测试的内容,即一级测评范围为300句,二级测评范围为600句,三级测评范围为900句。

　　为使学生更好地掌握外语口语,提高学生的外语综合应用能力,顺利通过应用外国语能力水平测试,我们开发出以公共英语和专业英语为主线的学生学习手册。该手册共有四册,配备音频资源,书中所配插图还可作为同学们看图说话的选题。第一册内容为公共场合用语;第二册内容为财经与旅游类用语;第三册内容为理工与医学类用语;第四册内容为外国经典名曲练唱100首。

　　"369PGT"学习模式旨在外语口语教学中注重突出语言实践,使学生在各类活动中进行学习。学生在学习过程中始终坚持自主合作探究学习。本系列学习手册的内容结构、活动形式、教学模式、教学方法等适用于学生课内外自主学习,从而建立起一套较为完整的符合实际的外语口语学习体系,以全面提高学生的外语应用能力及职业综合素质。

　　第一册《高职PGT英语口语教程》编写的基本思路清晰,以日常生活对话内容为主,进行必要补充、延伸和拓展,结合英语口语教学的重点,突出口语交际的特点,以情景对话为主,教材内容力求源于生活、再现生活,设置的情景是学生熟悉并感兴趣的,主要有校园篇、购物篇、银行篇、公共交通篇、旅行篇、餐饮篇、娱乐和文化篇、求职面试篇、公共安全篇,使学生能够通过观察情景,进入语境,产生兴趣,在有趣的对话练习表演中完成交际性语言学习任务。本教材在编写对话内容上尽可能满足每名学生的实际生活、工作需要,最大限度地切合每名学生的性格特点与生活经验,学习基础知识和文化背景,以促使学生主动学习。

　　由于时间仓促,加之编写者水平有限,本系列学习手册难免有不足之处,望老师、同学们在使用过程中提出宝贵意见,使其日趋完善。

《369PGT外语听说练习手册》编写组

2020年6月

目　　录

Part A Partner and Group .... (1)

Ⅰ. On the Campus 校园篇 .... (1)
   Situation 1: At English Corner 在英语角 .... (1)
   Situation 2: In the Library 在图书馆 .... (3)
   Situation 3: On the Playground 在操场 .... (4)
   Situation 4: In the Dining Hall 在食堂 .... (5)
   Situation 5: In the Dorm 在寝室 .... (7)
   Situation 6: At the Campus Clinic 在医务室 .... (8)
   Situation 7: In the Lab 在实验室 .... (9)

Ⅱ. Shopping 购物篇 .... (11)
   Situation 1: In the Home Shop 在家居店 .... (11)
   Situation 2: In the Bookstore 在书店 .... (13)
   Situation 3: In the Office Supplies Store 在办公用品商店 .... (13)
   Situation 4: Complaints and Suggestions 投诉及建议 .... (14)

Ⅲ. At the Bank 银行篇 .... (16)
   Situation 1: Open an Account 开户 .... (16)
   Situation 2: Withdraw Money 取款 .... (18)
   Situation 3: Money Exchange 货币兑换 .... (19)
   Situation 4: Loss Reporting 挂失 .... (20)

Ⅳ. Transportation 公共交通篇 .... (22)
   Situation 1: Booking an Air Ticket 订机票 .... (22)
   Situation 2: At the Check-in Counter 在登机手续柜台 .... (24)
   Situation 3: In the Luggage Claim Area 在行李提取区 .... (25)
   Situation 4: In the Subway 在地铁站 .... (25)
   Situation 5: In a Taxi 在出租车上 .... (27)
   Situation 6: At the Railway Station 在火车站 .... (28)
   Situation 7: Asking & Giving Directions 问路与指路 .... (30)

Ⅴ. Traveling 旅行篇 .... (33)
   Situation 1: At the Travel Agency 在旅行社 .... (33)
   Situation 2: Losing Luggage 行李遗失 .... (35)
   Situation 3: Packing for a Trip 旅行准备 .... (36)
   Situation 4: In a Duty-free Shop 在免税店 .... (37)

Situation 5：Sightseeing 观光 …………………………………………………… (38)
　　Situation 6：Asking Someone to Take a Picture 请人拍照 ……………………… (39)
　　Situation 7：Talking about Weather 谈论天气 ………………………………… (40)
　　Situation 8：At Customs 在海关 ………………………………………………… (41)
　　Situation 9：Interview for Visa Application 签证面谈 ………………………… (42)
Ⅵ. Catering 餐饮篇 ……………………………………………………………………… (44)
Ⅶ. Entertainment & Culture 娱乐和文化篇 …………………………………………… (48)
　　Situation 1：At the Cinema 在电影院 …………………………………………… (48)
　　Situation 2：At the Shanghai World Expo 在上海世博会 …………………… (50)
　　Situation 3：At the Museum 在博物馆 ………………………………………… (51)
　　Situation 4：At the Concert 在音乐厅 ………………………………………… (52)
　　Situation 5：At a Fashion Show 在时装秀 …………………………………… (54)
Ⅷ. Interview 求职面试篇 ………………………………………………………………… (57)
　　Situation 1：Self-introduction 自我介绍 ……………………………………… (57)
　　Situation 2：About Reason for Application 应聘理由 ………………………… (58)
　　Situation 3：About Work Experience 工作经验 ……………………………… (62)
　　Situation 4：About Strength & Achievements 优点和成绩 …………………… (64)
　　Situation 5：About Characteristics 谈论性格 ………………………………… (66)
Ⅸ. Public Security 公共安全篇 ………………………………………………………… (68)
　　Situation 1：Reporting a Crime 报案 …………………………………………… (68)
　　Situation 2：Health and Safety 健康与安全 …………………………………… (70)

Part B　Group and Team …………………………………………………………… (72)
　Test 1 ………………………………………………………………………………… (72)
　Test 2 ………………………………………………………………………………… (74)
　Test 3 ………………………………………………………………………………… (76)
　Test 4 ………………………………………………………………………………… (78)
　Test 5 ………………………………………………………………………………… (80)
　Test 6 ………………………………………………………………………………… (82)
　Test 7 ………………………………………………………………………………… (84)
　Test 8 ………………………………………………………………………………… (86)
　Test 9 ………………………………………………………………………………… (88)
　Test 10 ……………………………………………………………………………… (90)
　Test 11 ……………………………………………………………………………… (92)
　Test 12 ……………………………………………………………………………… (94)

Vocabulary …………………………………………………………………………… (97)

Part A Partner and Group

Ⅰ. On the Campus 校园篇

In this chapter, campus life is set as the background. It includes some commonly used expressions according to different situations encountered in campus life, such as the English corner, the library, the playground, the dining hall, the dorm, the campus clinic, and the lab.

校园篇以学生们熟悉的校园生活场景,如在英语角、图书馆、操场、食堂、寝室、医务室、实验室的常见对话为主要内容,在口语练习过程中学生们可采取对话练习、表演等方式进行学习。应注意发音准确,语调自然。

Situation 1: At English Corner 在英语角

1. Alex(exchange student): Hi, how do you do?

Li Hong(Chinese student): How do you do?

2. Alex: Allow me to introduce myself. My name is Alex.

Li Hong: Nice to meet you, Alex. I'm Li Hong. I'd like to introduce you to my friend Helen.

3. Helen(exchange student): Hi, I'm Helen. I'm pleased to meet you.

Alex: Nice to meet you. Are you from America, too?

Helen: No, I'm from England.

4. Alex: Oh, the Olympic Games has just been hosted in London. Have you been there to watch it?

Helen: Yes, I have. Actually I used to be there as an interpreter for a few days. You know, I can speak both English and Chinese.

5. Alex: Good for you! Then you must have seen the gorgeous opening ceremony, right?

Helen: Yes, and I was arranged to interpret for some Chinese personnel.

6. Alex:Wow,you must be an old Chinese hand! How long have you been in China?

Helen:I've been studying in China for 5 years.

7. Helen:Have you got adapted here,Alex?

Alex:En,I think so. One year ago when I just came here,I used to feel hungry because I disliked the food.

8. Helen:Chinese food is much different from western food. But I think it is delicious. Now you still hate it?

Alex:Now I've got to love Chinese food including fried noodles,dumplings,roast duck and so on.

9. Li Hong:There will be an activity about food culture next week. Would you like to take part in it?

Helen:Wonderful,we can get to know more about your customs.

Alex:Yes,and we can make more friends,too!

10. Li Hong:It's 9 o'clock. We've to go back.

Helen:Yes,time for bed.

11. Alex:See you tomorrow.

Li Hong:See you and good night!

1. 亚历克斯(交换生):你好!

李红(中国学生):你好!

2. 亚历克斯:自我介绍一下,我叫亚历克斯。

李红:很高兴认识你,亚历克斯,我是李红,让我来介绍你和我的朋友海伦认识吧。

3. 海伦(交换生):你好,我是海伦,很高兴认识你。

亚历克斯:很高兴认识你,你也来自美国吗?

海伦:不,我来自英国。

4. 亚历克斯:哦,奥运会刚在伦敦举行,你去那里看比赛了吗?

海伦:是的,我去了。实际上我还在那里做了几天译员,我会说中文和英文。

5. 亚历克斯:好样的,那你一定看了宏伟壮观的开幕式吧?

海伦:是的,我还被安排给一些中国工作人员当翻译呢。

6. 亚历克斯:哇,那你一定是一个中国通了! 你在中国待了多久了?

海伦:我在中国留学5年了。

7. 海伦:你是否适应了这里?

亚历克斯:嗯,差不多。一年前我刚来中国时总是饿肚子,因为我不喜欢这里的食物。

8. 海伦:中国食物与西方食物有很大不同,但我觉得很好吃。你现在还讨厌它吗?

亚历克斯:现在我渐渐爱上了中国食物,包括炒面、饺子、烤鸭等。

9. 李红:下周有一个关于食品文化的活动,你们愿意来参加吗?

海伦:太好了,我们可以更多地了解你们的风俗。

亚历克斯:是的,我们还能交更多的朋友。

10. 李红:现在九点了,要回去了。

海伦:是的,该就寝了。

11. 亚历克斯:明天见。

李红:再见! 晚安!

Situation 2:In the Library 在图书馆

1. David:I'd like to know how to use the student ID card. Could you help me please?

Librarian:Of course. You can use your student ID card to borrow books and read magazines in the library.

2. David:How many books am I allowed to check out at a time?

Librarian:You can borrow up to five books at a time. But you can't check out magazines or journals;they have to be read in the library.

3. David:How long can I keep the books?

Librarian:For one month. If you don't return a book in time,you'll be fined. But if you renew them,you can keep them longer.

4. David:I want to borrow two books on Chinese literature and two novels. Can you show me where I can find them?

Librarian:Yes,over there on your right.

5. Librarian:Hi! Can I help you?

David:I'd like to return these books,please.

6. Librarian:OK. Are these books all yours?

David:Yes. Four in all.

7. Librarian:I'm afraid you have to pay a fine.

David:Do I? How much?

Librarian:1 yuan.

1. 大卫:我想知道怎样使用学生证借书,你能帮我吗?

图书管理员:当然了。你只要有学生证,就能从图书馆借书,在图书馆里阅读杂志。

2. 大卫:一次可以借几本书?

图书管理员:一次五本。但杂志或期刊是不能外借的,你只能在图书馆里阅读。

3. 大卫:我可以借多长时间?

图书管理员:一个月。如果你不按时还书就会被罚款,但如果你办理续借,就可以保留更长时间。

4. 大卫:我现在想借两本有关中国文学的书和两本小说。你能告诉我在哪儿可以找到吗?

图书管理员:可以。在你右边。

5. 图书管理员:要帮忙吗?

大卫:我想还这些书。

6. 图书管理员:好的。这些全是你借的吗?

大卫:是的。总共4本。

7. 图书管理员:恐怕你要付罚款了。

大卫:是吗?罚多少钱?

图书管理员:1元。

Situation 3:On the Playground 在操场

1. John:Would you like to go for a run?

Marry:Great,where would you like to go?

2. John:We could go to the playground. There shouldn't be many people there now.

Marry:Good. Just let me get changed.

3. John:How do you feel after jogging?

Marry:Oh,I feel really tired and sweaty.

4. John:But it'll help you keep fit.

Marry:Sure. More importantly,I can have peace of mind.

5. John:How about going for a bike ride?

Marry:Sure. Where to go?

6. John:Let's call Harry and ask him. He always knows the best places to go.

Marry: That's a good idea. I'll get ready.

7. John: Which do you like to play, basketball, volleyball, badminton, football, tennis or table tennis?

Marry: Well, I prefer volleyball, because I admire Lang Ping very much.

1. 约翰:你想去跑步吗?

玛丽:好啊。你想去哪儿跑步?

2. 约翰:我们去操场吧。现在那儿应该没多少人。

玛丽:好的。等我换件衣服。

3. 约翰:练习慢跑感觉怎么样?

玛丽:哦,感觉好累,还出了很多汗。

4. 约翰:但是慢跑帮助你保持健康。

玛丽:当然了。最重要的是还可以有个平和的心态。

5. 约翰:骑自行车出去怎么样?

玛丽:可以啊。去哪儿?

6. 约翰:我们打电话给哈里叫他一起去吧。他知道骑车去哪儿最好。

玛丽:好主意。马上准备。

7. 约翰:你喜欢哪种球类运动,篮球、排球、羽毛球、足球、网球还是乒乓球?

玛丽:呃,我喜欢排球,因为我很钦佩郎平。

Situation 4: In the Dining Hall 在食堂

1. Waiter: Have you decided what you'd like?

Marry: Yeah! First I'll have a glass of tomato juice.

2. Waiter: And then?

Marry: I'll have the lamb chops, well-done, please.

3. Waiter: How about you? What would you like to eat?

Susan: Well, I think I'll try the pancakes.

4. Waiter: And would you like some drinks, such as fruit juice or coffee?

Susan: I think I'd like a cup of coffee.

5. Waiter: Aren't you going to have some dessert? We have egg tart, small cakes, and ice cream.

Marry:Egg tart sounds good,doesn't it?

Susan:It's delicious. That's just what I want.

6. Waiter:Will you eat here or take away?

Marry:To eat here.

1. 服务员:你想好点什么了吗?

玛丽:是的。先要一杯番茄汁。

2. 服务员:然后呢?

玛丽:我要一份羊排,全熟。

3. 服务员:你呢? 你想吃点什么?

苏珊:呃,我想试一下薄饼。

4. 服务员:你想喝点什么吗? 例如果汁或者咖啡?

苏珊:我想点杯咖啡。

5. 服务员:不再来点甜点吗? 我们有蛋挞、小蛋糕和冰激凌。

玛丽:蛋挞听起来不错,不是吗?

苏珊:很美味,那也是我想要的。

6. 服务员:在这里吃还是带走?

玛丽:在这儿吃。

1. Marry:I don't feel like eating in our canteen today. How about eating out in a western restaurant?

Susan:I love eating out,but I'm not such a fan of western food.

2. Marry:Are you kidding? Everyone loves beefsteak, hamburger, pizza and spaghetti.

Susan:Well,not me.

3. Marry:Then,what about a Chinese restaurant? We can order Beijing roast duck, gongbao chicken,sweet and sour fillet of pork,bouilli or tomato soup with egg.

Susan:Sounds wonderful. After that,we can also go for a cup of coffee and have some snacks.

Marry:It makes my mouth water. Let's go now.

1. 玛丽:我今天不太想在学校食堂吃饭。我们到西餐厅吃,怎么样?

苏珊:我喜欢下馆子,但是我不太喜欢西餐。

2. 玛丽:你在开玩笑吧?每个人都喜欢吃牛排、汉堡、比萨和意大利面。

苏珊:呃,我不喜欢。

3. 玛丽:那么,去中餐厅怎么样?我们可以点北京烤鸭、宫保鸡丁、糖醋里脊、红烧肉或者番茄蛋汤。

苏珊:听起来不错。吃完我们还可以去喝杯咖啡,吃点零食。

玛丽:我的口水都要流出来了,我们马上走吧。

Situation 5: In the Dorm 在寝室

1. Mary: How is your new dorm?

Ann: It's very nice. I have three roommates, and they are very kind and friendly.

2. Mary: Well, do you all major in the same subject?

Ann: No, the other girls major in computer science, so they can help me a lot with my computer operating.

Mary: That's great!

3. Carl: Hey, Jim, wake up and get out of bed.

Jim: Do I have to get up now?

4. Carl: You'd better get up, or you'll be late.

Jim: What are you talking about? My alarm hasn't even gone off yet.

5. Carl: Yes, it has. It went off 30 minutes ago. You slept right through it. You were sleeping like a log.

Jim: I must have slept right through it.

6. Carl: The early bird gets the worm.

Jim: I know. But I don't want any worms.

Carl: If you don't make an effort now, later on it'll be a lot tougher for you.

7. Adam: Would you like to go skating with me this afternoon?

Bruce: Oh, I'd love to. But we're going to clean our dormitory. I can't be absent.

1. 玛丽:你的新宿舍怎么样?

安:挺好的。有三个室友,她们都非常善良友好。

2. 玛丽:嗯,那你们都是一个专业的吗?

安:不是的,她们三人的专业是计算机科学,她们在电脑操作上能帮我很多忙呢。

玛丽:那太好了!

3. 卡尔:嘿,吉姆,醒醒,起床了。

吉姆:我现在一定得起来吗?

4. 卡尔:你最好起来,不然就迟到了。

吉姆:你在说什么?我闹钟还没响呢。

5. 卡尔:响了。30分钟前就响了。你睡过了。你睡得太沉了。

吉姆:那我肯定是睡过了。

6. 卡尔:早起的鸟儿有虫吃。

吉姆:我知道。但我可不想吃虫子。

卡尔:如果你现在不赶紧起来,一会就更难起来了。

7. 亚当:下午跟我一起去溜冰吧?

布鲁斯:噢,我很乐意去。但是我们下午要打扫宿舍,我不能缺席。

Situation 6:At the Campus Clinic 在医务室

1. Doctor:What's wrong with you,young man?

Jim:I cough a great deal at night.

2. Doctor:How long have you been like this?

Jim:About a week. Sometimes I have a fever.

3. Doctor:Let me listen to your lungs...Well,I think you'd better go and have your chest X-rayed.

Jim:OK.

4. Doctor:What's the matter with you?

Blake:Recently I feel very tired,and I have no appetite.

5. Doctor:What about your sleep?

Blake:Very bad.

6. Doctor:Now let me examine you...Well,there's nothing serious with you. Do you get much exercise?

Blake:No,I seem to have no time for exercise now. Doctor,can you give me some medicine to help me to sleep?

7. Doctor:Yes,but you need to do some exercise.

Blake: Thank you, doctor. I'll follow your advice.

1. 医生:怎么了,年轻人?

吉姆:我晚上咳嗽得很厉害。

2. 医生:像这样多长时间了?

吉姆:大约一周。有时候还发烧。

3. 医生:让我听听你的肺……我看,你还是去做一下胸部透视吧。

吉姆:好吧。

4. 医生:你怎么了?

布莱克:最近我感到很疲倦,并且没什么胃口。

5. 医生:你的睡眠怎么样?

布莱克:很不好。

6. 医生:现在让我给你检查一下……哦,你没什么大问题,你经常锻炼身体吗?

布莱克:不,我现在似乎没时间进行锻炼。医生,你能给我开点助我入眠的药吗?

7. 医生:可以,但是你也需要锻炼身体。

布莱克:谢谢你,医生。我听你的。

Situation 7: In the Lab 在实验室

1. Teacher: Good afternoon, everyone. The experiment is to start at 3 o'clock. Have you gone through the instructions?

Students: Yes, sir.

2. Teacher: OK. Now some points for attention. First of all, pay attention to safety... Now, sign your names on the lab record, and after that you can start. If there are any questions, just let me know.

Peter: Excuse me, sir. This air compressor doesn't work.

3. Teacher: Have you turned it on?

Peter: Yes, I have.

4. Teacher: OK. I'll get you another one.

Peter: Thank you.

1. 老师:各位同学下午好。实验3点开始。大家都看了操作说明吗?

学生们:看了,老师。

2. 老师:好。需要注意几点。首先,注意安全……现在,在实验记录簿上签名,然后就可以开始了。如果有任何问题,跟我说。

彼得:打扰一下,老师。这个空气压缩机坏了。

3. 老师:你打开了吗?

彼得:打开了。

4. 老师:好吧。我另外再拿一个给你。

彼得:谢谢。

Ⅱ. Shopping 购物篇

In this chapter, shopping is set as the background. It includes some commonly used dialogues according to different situations, such as in the department store, in the bookstore, in the electronic goods store and complaints and suggestions.

购物篇的情景对话以商场、书店、电子产品商店为主要对话场景,涉及购物过程中的问路、失物招领、投诉建议等常见对话,在口语练习过程中学生们可采取对话练习、表演等方式进行学习。应注意发音准确,语调自然。请看下面的情景对话:

Situation 1:In the Home Shop 在家居店

1. Salesman:Good morning. What can I do for you?

Tom:I'm looking for a sofa. Can you recommend one for me?

2. Salesman: Sure. How about this one? It features fancy colors and innovative design. It is very popular among young people.

Tom:Wow,the color is really attractive. It goes well with my living room.

3. Salesman:And it is on sale now. You can't miss it.

Tom:Really? How much is it?

4. Salesman:4,999 yuan.

Tom:OK. I'll take it.

5. Salesman:How would you like to pay? Cash or credit card?

Tom:Credit card,please.

1. 销售员:早上好,请问有什么可以帮您的吗?

汤姆:我想买沙发,可以帮我推荐吗?

2. 销售员:当然,您看这款怎么样? 它不仅色彩丰富,而且设计很有创意,在年轻人当中很受欢迎。

汤姆:嗯,颜色确实很迷人,和我家客厅的风格很搭配。

3. 销售员:这款现在正在做活动。机不可失哦。

汤姆:真的吗? 多少钱?

4. 销售员:4999 元。

顾客:好的。就它了。

5. 销售员:请问您是付现金还是刷信用卡?

汤姆:刷信用卡。

Dialogue 1—Lost and Found 失物招领

1. Tom:Excuse me. I've got a problem. I think I've lost my wallet.

Salesman:Are you sure it's not in your bag?

Tom:Yes. I have checked carefully.

2. Salesman:Why don't you check at the Lost and Found Office?

Tom:That's a good idea. Thank you.

1. 汤姆:劳驾,我遇到点问题。我丢了钱包。

销售员:您肯定包里没有吗?

汤姆:没有。我已经仔细地找过了。

2. 销售员:您为何不去失物招领处询问呢?

汤姆:好主意。谢谢。

Dialogue 2—Asking for Directions 问路

1. Tom:Excuse me. Could you tell me where the toilet is please?

Jack:I'm sorry. I'm a stranger here too. Why not ask at Enquiries?

2. Tom:Thank you. But how can I get to the Enquiries Counter?

Jack:Oh, that's easy. Walk to the corner, and then turn left. You will find a big sign over there.

3. Tom:Thanks a lot.

Jack:You're welcome. Good luck.

1. 汤姆:劳驾,请问洗手间在哪儿?

杰克:不好意思。我对这里也不熟。您去服务台问问吧。

2. 汤姆:谢谢您。请问服务台怎么去呢?

杰克:很容易找到的。直走到头,然后左拐。那儿有一个很大的标识牌。

3. 汤姆:谢谢您。

杰克:不客气。祝您顺利。

Situation 2: In the Bookstore 在书店

1. Sales Clerk: We're having a sale in our store. Would you like to buy something?

Jack: I want to buy the 2nd edition of this book.

2. Sales Clerk: We have books on politics, economy, culture, history, art, etc. You can find whatever you want.

Jack: Okay, let me see, I want to buy these two books on history.

Sales Clerk: Okay, the total price is 65 yuan.

3. Sales Clerk: I'm sorry this book is out of stock. It's a bestseller now.

Jack: OK, please reserve me a copy and call me when it arrives.

4. Jack: I was wondering whether you have any of Jane Austen's books?

Sales Clerk: Hold on please, let me check.

5. Jack: I want to buy some books on economics. Where can I find them?

Sales Clerk: Economics books are on the left shelves, and the recently published ones are on the counter in the middle.

1. 店员：我们书店正在做活动，你想买点什么？

杰克：我想买这本书的第二版。

2. 店员：我们有政治、经济、文化、历史、艺术等各方面的书籍，您一定能找到您要的。

杰克：好的，我想买这两本建筑方面的书。

店员：好的，这两本书的总价是65元。

3. 店员：很抱歉这本书已经卖完了，它现在是最畅销的书。

杰克：好的，如果新书到了，请留一本，并联系我。

4. 杰克：不知道您这里有没有简·奥斯汀的书。

店员：请稍等，我帮您查一下。

5. 杰克：我想买经济方面的书，请问在哪里？

店员：经济方面的书在左边书架上，并且最新出版的在中间的柜台上。

Situation 3: In the Office Supplies Store 在办公用品商店

1. Salesman: Good morning. What can I do for you?

Tom: I'd like to order 2 filing cabinets in white. The catalogue number is 90CF.

2. Salesman: When do you want it?

Tom: Can you deliver it tomorrow?

3. Salesman: No problem.

Tom: OK. I also need some small articles, such as paper clips, clear tapes, erasers and sticky notes.

4. Salesman: Would you please make a list of all the articles you need?

Tom: OK. Wait a moment.

5. Salesman: By the way, do you have any special requests?

Tom: Oh, yes. You've reminded me of something. The pens we are using are poor in quality. Can you recommend some good brands for me?

Salesman: Okay, this way, please.

1. 销售员:早上好,请问有什么可以帮您的吗?

汤姆:我想订购两个白色的文件柜。目录编号是90CF。

2. 销售员:您什么时候需要?

汤姆:明天可以送达吗?

3. 销售员:没问题。

汤姆:好的,我还要一些小物品,比如纸夹、透明胶、橡皮擦和便利贴。

4. 销售员:您可以把您要买的东西列一份清单给我吗?

汤姆:好的,请稍等。

5. 销售员:顺便问一下,您还有什么特别的要求吗?

汤姆:哦,您提醒了我。我们现在用的笔质量很差。可以推荐一些好的品牌吗?

销售员:好的,这边请。

Situation 4: Complaints and Suggestions 投诉及建议

1. Sales Clerk: What is your trouble?

Lucy: I'm afraid I have bad news for you. The woolen sweaters you delivered do not match the sample we provided.

Sales Clerk: I am sorry for the problem we have caused you. Let me check on this and get back to you tomorrow.

2. Sales Clerk: Hello. What can I do for you?

Lucy: I bought a book here yesterday, and I want to exchange it because it has a problem.

Sales Clerk: Could you please tell me what the problem is?

Lucy: Well, the printing on the last pages is very poor, I can't read it.

Sales Clerk: Really? Let me have a look... I'm really sorry for this problem. I will exchange it right now.

3. Purchaser: I'd like to make a complaint about your products. The parts are of poor quality and workmanship.

Salesman: Please accept my apology on behalf of our company. I'll contact our manager right away.

Purchaser: I hope that you can tackle this problem as soon as possible.

1. 店员:您有什么问题?

露西:恐怕对你来说是个坏消息。你们发送的羊毛衫和我们提供的样品不符。

店员:我非常抱歉给您带来的麻烦。请让我查查看,明天再回复您。

2. 店员:您好,您有什么需要吗?

露西:我昨天在这儿买的书有问题,想换一下。

店员:您能告诉我,书有什么问题吗?

露西:后面几页印得很模糊,根本看不清。

店员:真的吗?让我看一下……这个问题我真的很抱歉。我马上为您换货。

3. 采购员:我要投诉你们的产品。那些零部件质量和工艺都很差。

销售员:我代表公司向您致歉,请您接受。我会马上联系经理。

采购员:我希望你们可以尽快处理这件事。

Ⅲ. At the Bank 银行篇

In this chapter, business at the bank is set as the background. It includes some commonly used dialogues according to different business conducted, such as opening an account, withdrawing money, money exchange and loss reporting.

银行篇为我们在银行中进行一系列活动包括开户、取钱、兑换外币、挂失提供了鲜活的情景对话。在口语练习过程中，学生们可采取对话练习、表演等方式熟练掌握并灵活运用以下对话内容：

Situation 1:Open an Account 开户

1. Bank Clerk:May I help you?

Tom:Yes,I would like to open an account.

2. Bank Clerk:A current account or deposit account?

Tom:I am not sure. Could you please tell me the difference between the two types?

3. Bank Clerk:Usually, current accounts are more convenient. There is no limits on withdrawing money;you can make withdrawals any time you like.

Tom:What about deposit accounts?

4. Bank Clerk:They have limitations on withdrawing money. You can only make withdrawals according to the terms of your account, but the interest of deposit accounts is a little higher than that of current accounts.

Tom:Well,I have monthly remittances from my parents and I would like to have the money paid into an account.

5. Bank Clerk:Then you'd better open a current account. The bank will give you a deposit card and you can take out money whenever you like.

Tom:OK. What do I have to do?

6. Bank Clerk:Just fill in this application form. Do you have your ID card with you?

Tom:Yes,here you are.

7. Bank Clerk:Please wait a moment. I can help you immediately.

Tom:Thank you very much.

8. Bank Clerk:Please choose a password and input it.

Tom: OK.

9. Bank Clerk: OK, your current account is now available. Anything else I can help you with?

Tom: Thank you. I would also like access to online banking.

10. Bank Clerk: So first, please log on our bank's official website, register your account, fill in the information details and then set your account password. For the verification code, our system will then send it to your mobile phone. That's all.

Tom: Oh. That's easy enough.

11. Bank Clerk: Yes, let's come back to your account, if everything is correct, please sign at the bottom as confirmation.

Tom: Let me see. Yeah, it is correct, here you are.

12. Bank Clerk: Please take your cards and transaction records with you. Could you rate my service?

Tom: Of course, very satisfied.

1. 银行职员：请问您需要什么帮助？

汤姆：我想开个银行账户。

2. 银行职员：活期存款账户还是定期存款账户？

汤姆：我不确定。请问二者有什么区别？

3. 银行职员：一般来说，活期存款账户更加方便，它没有取款限制，您可以随时取款。

汤姆：那定期存款账户呢？

4. 银行职员：定期存款账户有取款时间限制，到期才可以取，但是利息比活期要高。

汤姆：这样啊。我父母每个月会给我汇款，我需要一个账户来收款。

5. 银行职员：那您最好办理活期存款账户，您会拥有一张银行的储蓄卡，随时可以取钱。

汤姆：好的。那要如何申请？

6. 银行职员：您只需要填写这份申请表。您带身份证了吗？

汤姆：带了，给您。

7. 银行职员：请稍等，我马上帮您办理。

汤姆：非常感谢。

8. 银行职员：请输入密码。

汤姆：好的。

9. 银行职员:好了,您的账户已经开通。请问还需要其他帮助吗?

汤姆:谢谢! 我想开通网上银行。

10. 银行职员:首先,您需要登录我们的官方网站,点击注册申请,输入详细的账户信息,设置账户密码。我们的系统会将验证码发至您的手机,通过输入验证码就可以完成。

汤姆:哦,这么简单啊。

11. 银行职员:是的。我们再核对一下账户信息。如果无误,请在下栏签字确认。

汤姆:我看看。对的。签好了,给您。

12. 银行职员:请收好您的银行卡及业务凭证。请您对本次服务做出评价。

汤姆:好的,非常满意。

Situation 2:Withdraw Money 取款

1. Bank Clerk:Good morning. Is there anything I can do for you?

Tom:Yes,would you please help me withdraw some money from my account.

2. Bank Clerk:You can do it on the Automatic Teller Machine near the gate.

Tom:I'm sorry. I don't know how to operate it.

3. Bank Clerk:OK. Can you give me your debit card?

Tom:Here it is.

4. Bank Clerk:Input your PIN number,please.

Tom:OK.

5. Bank Clerk:The balance is 2000 RMB. You can input the amount you are going to withdraw.

Tom:500 RMB.

6. Bank Clerk:Well,here is your cash,transaction record and card.

Tom:Thank you.

1. 银行职员:上午好,请问您需要什么帮助?

汤姆:您好,您能不能帮我办理取钱业务?

2. 银行职员:您可以到门口的自助取款机取钱。

汤姆:不好意思,我不知道怎么操作。

3. 银行职员:没关系,麻烦把银行借记卡给我一下。

汤姆:给您。

4. 银行职员:请输入密码。

汤姆:好的。

5. 银行职员:您的余额为2000元。请您输入取款金额。

汤姆:500元。

6. 银行职员:已取好,这是您的现金、小票和您的银行卡。

汤姆:谢谢。

Situation 3:Money Exchange 货币兑换

1. Bank Clerk:How can I help you?

Tom:I'd like to change some money.

2. Bank Clerk:What sort of currency do you want to exchange,sir?

Tom:Hong Kong dollars. What's the exchange rate today please?

3. Bank Clerk:Today's rate is 1 RMB for 1.1937. How much would you like to change?

Tom:1000 RMB if I may. Here you are.

4. Bank Clerk:This is an exchange record. Please fill in your name, ID number and the amount you want to change.

Tom:All right. Here it is.

5. Bank Clerk:Here is the 1193.7 HKD and the exchange record. Please check it.

Tom:It's alright,thanks very much.

1. 银行职员:请问需要什么帮助?

汤姆:我想兑换货币。

2. 银行职员:那您要兑换哪种货币?

汤姆:港币。今天汇率是多少?

3. 银行职员:今天人民币兑港币的汇率为1∶1.1937。您打算兑换多少金额?

汤姆:1000元人民币。

4. 银行职员:这是兑换单据,请您填写姓名、身份证号以及兑换金额。

汤姆:好的,已填好。

5. 银行职员:这是1193.7港币和兑换小票,请您核查。

汤姆:没问题,谢谢。

Situation 4: Loss Reporting 挂失

1. Tom: Excuse me, I have lost my bank card.

Bank Clerk: Is it a deposit card or a credit card?

2. Tom: A deposit card.

Bank Clerk: Would you please tell me how much money in it?

3. Tom: About 8000 yuan.

Bank Clerk: OK. Please tell me your name, address and account number.

4. Tom: My name is Tom, my address is NO 1. Minzhu Road, Wuchang District of Wuhan. But I cannot remember my account number.

Bank Clerk: Don't worry, sir. Let me check it. Wait a minute, please. I've checked out your account number. The balance of your account is still 8000 yuan.

5. Tom: Thank goodness! My money is still there. Thank you!

Bank Clerk: You're welcome. Please fill in a lost report, and write down the password you set when opening the account.

6. Bank Clerk: Have you finished the report? Don't forget to sign your name at the bottom.

Tom: I've done it. Here it is.

7. Bank Clerk: Well, your account will be frozen temporarily based on your application and ID certificate. Would you like a new card now?

Tom: Yes, I would. I need my balance transferred to the new card.

8. Bank Clerk: Please fill in an application form and give me 10 yuan for an annual fee.

Tom: Here you go.

9. Bank Clerk: OK, here is your new card. Please keep it safe.

Tom: Thank you.

1. 汤姆:打扰一下,我的银行卡丢了。

银行职员:是储蓄卡还是信用卡?

2. 汤姆:储蓄卡。

银行职员:您能告诉我您存了多少钱吗?

3. 汤姆:大约 8000 元人民币。

银行职员:好的,请告诉我您的姓名、地址和账号。

4. 汤姆:我叫汤姆,地址是武汉市武昌区民主路 1 号,但是我想不起来账号了。

银行职员:先生不用着急,让我查一下,请稍等。我查到了您的账号,您账户余额确实是人民币 8000 元。

5. 汤姆:谢天谢地,钱还在。谢谢!

银行职员:不用谢。请填写银行卡挂失单,然后写明您开户时使用的密码。

6. 银行职员:表填好了吗?记得在签名处签名。

汤姆:已经填好,您看看。

7. 银行职员:好的,根据您的个人申请和身份证件,您的账号已被暂时冻结。您需要办理一张新卡吗?

汤姆:是的。我需要把余额转入新卡。

8. 银行职员:请填写申请表,并交 10 元年费。

汤姆:给您。

9. 银行职员:这是您的新卡,请保管好。

汤姆:谢谢。

Ⅳ. Transportation 公共交通篇

This part includes situational dialogues about taking public transportation which concern taking a flight at an airport, taking a train at a railway station, taking a subway and taking a taxi, asking and giving directions.

公共交通篇以在日常交通中的订机票、在登机处、在行李提取处、在地铁站、在出租车上、在火车站、问路和指路为主要对话场景。口语练习过程中,学生们可采取对话练习、表演等方式进行学习。应注意发音准确,语调自然。请看下面的情景对话:

Situation 1:Booking an Air Ticket 订机票

1. Clerk:Good morning. What can I do for you?

2. Peter:I'd like to book a ticket.

3. Clerk:Sure,where are you going?

4. Peter:I want to go to Paris on May 1st.

5. Clerk:Do you want a direct flight?

6. Peter:Yes,I want to fly non-stop.

7. Clerk:Just a moment,please. Sorry,the non-stop flight on May 1st is fully booked. But there is an indirect flight available with one layover. It departs Wuhan at 19:00.

8. Peter:How long is the flight?

9. Clerk:The flight from Wuhan to Kunming is 3 hours,and the connecting flight to Paris is another 13 hours. So you will arrive in Paris at 7:00 the next day. These are all local times.

10. Peter:What is the layover time?

11. Clerk:You have 3 hours to make the connecting flight.

12. Peter:I guess I'll have to take this one.

13. Clerk:OK,first class or economy?

14. Peter:Economy and an aisle seat please. How much is the fare?

15. Clerk:One way or round trip?

16. Peter:One way trip.

17. Clerk:Economy fare for one way trip is 3900 yuan. Will you pay by cash or credit

card?

18. Peter: By credit card. Here you are.

19. Clerk: Thanks. May I see your passport, please?

20. Peter: Here it is.

21. Clerk: Thank you. Keep the receipt, please. Here's your passport and your ticket.

22. Peter: Thank you very much.

1. 职员:早上好！请问有什么需要帮助的吗?

2. 彼得:我想订一张机票。

3. 职员:好的。请问您要买到哪里的机票?

4. 彼得:我打算5月1号去巴黎。

5. 职员:您是要直航吗?

6. 彼得:是的,我要直飞的。

7. 职员:请稍等片刻。抱歉,5月1号去巴黎的直飞航班机票已订满了,不过当天还有一趟非直航的航班,中途要转机一次,晚上7点在武汉起飞。

8. 彼得:要飞多久?

9. 职员:从武汉到昆明要3个小时,从昆明到巴黎要13个小时。您会在第二天早上7点到达巴黎。以上时间都为当地时间。

10. 彼得:转机时间要多久?

11. 职员:3个小时。

12. 彼得:看来只能选这趟了。

13. 职员:好的,请问您要头等舱还是经济舱?

14. 彼得:经济舱靠走道的位置。请问多少钱?

15. 职员:您是要单程票还是往返票?

16. 彼得:单程票。

17. 职员:单程票经济舱的票价是3900元。请问您是付现金还是刷卡?

18. 彼得:刷卡。这是我的卡。

19. 职员:谢谢！请给我您的护照。

20. 彼得:这是我的护照。

21. 职员:谢谢！请拿好您的收据、护照和机票。

22. 彼得:非常感谢！

Situation 2: At the Check-in Counter 在登机手续柜台

1. Clerk: Good afternoon. What can I do for you?
2. Peter: Hi, is this the counter for flight MU2455 to London?
3. Clerk: Yes. May I have your ticket and passport?
4. Peter: This is my passport and e-ticket. Could I have a window seat?
5. Clerk: OK. How many items of luggage would you like to check in?
6. Peter: I have 3 items in all.
7. Clerk: Would you please put your luggage on the scale?
8. Peter: OK. Is that inside the free allowance?
9. Clerk: Yes, we allow twenty kilos each. Any carry-ons?
10. Peter: Yes, I've got a small bag with me. By the way, could I take perfume on a plane?
11. Clerk: Sorry, explosives like perfume are not allowed. But you can put them in your checked luggage.
12. Peter: What about the portable battery charger?
13. Clerk: It's OK. Here are your ticket, passport, boarding pass and your luggage claim tag.
14. Peter: Thank you.
15. Clerk: You're welcome.

1. 职员：下午好！请问您需要什么帮助？
2. 彼得：你好！这里是办理飞往伦敦的 MU2455 航班登机手续的柜台吗？
3. 职员：是的。请出示您的机票和护照。
4. 彼得：这是我的护照和电子机票。可以给我选个靠窗的位置吗？
5. 职员：好的。您有多少件行李需要托运？
6. 彼得：我有 3 件。
7. 职员：请把行李放到秤上。
8. 彼得：好的。这没超出免费行李限额吧？
9. 职员：是的。每人限 20 千克。有随身携带的物品吗？
10. 彼得：有一个小背包。对了，飞机上我能带香水吗？

11. 职员:抱歉,像香水这样的易爆物品不能带到飞机上。但是您可以放进托运的行李中。
12. 彼得:那便携式充电器呢?
13. 职员:可以的。这是您的机票、护照、登机牌和行李牌。
14. 彼得:谢谢!
15. 职员:不客气!

Situation 3:In the Luggage Claim Area 在行李提取区

1. Peter:Excuse me. Where can I get my luggage?

2. Airport Staff:Go down this escalator. It's just downstairs.

3. Peter:Excuse me, sir. I arrived from Wuhan on flight MU2455. On which carousel is the luggage from this flight?

4. Airport Staff:You can check the flight display board above each carousel. The information on your baggage claim stub will help you get your luggage.

5. Peter:Where can I find a baggage cart?

6. Airport Staff:They're over there.

7. Peter:Thank you very much.

1. 彼得:抱歉打扰一下,请问取行李的地方在哪里?
2. 机场工作人员:坐这个电梯下去就到了,就在楼下。
3. 彼得:抱歉打扰了,我从武汉飞来,乘坐的是 MU2455 航班,请问对应的行李传送带是哪一条?
4. 机场工作人员:您可以查看每条传送带上电子显示屏里的信息。行李提取存根上的信息可以帮您找到自己的行李。
5. 彼得:哪里有行李推车?
6. 机场工作人员:就在那边。
7. 彼得:非常感谢!

Situation 4:In the Subway 在地铁站

1. Mary:Excuse me. I wonder if you could help me. I'm looking for the Dream Building.

Tom: You're lost, poor little girl. It's across the city.

2. Mary: Really? Oh my God. Then where am I now?

Tom: Do you have a map?

Mary: Yes, I do have a map. Here it is.

3. Tom: This is Peking Times Square. This is the bus station. We are here. See?

Mary: I see. How can I get to the Dream Building?

Tom: You can take a taxi there. Tell the taxi driver your destination and he will take you there.

4. Mary: Low-carbon travel is advocated nowadays, so I prefer to take a bus or subway. Where is the nearest subway station?

Tom: The nearest subway station is on the corner of Jianwai SOHO, next to the library.

5. Mary: How can I get to the subway station?

Tom: You can take bus No. 40 just right there. Get off at the CBD station. You'll find an entrance to the subway.

Mary: Then?

Tom: Dream Building is around Gucheng Station. So you can take subway Line 2 to Chongwenmen station and then transfer to Line 5 to Gucheng station. You will find the Dream Building on your right after you come out of the station.

6. Mary: OK, thank you very much for your help.

Tom: You're welcome.

1. 玛丽：打扰一下，你能帮帮我吗？我在找梦想大厦。

汤姆：你迷路了，可怜的小姑娘，它在城的那边呢。

2. 玛丽：真的吗？我的天呀！那我现在在哪儿呢？

汤姆：你有地图吗？

玛丽：我有，给你。

3. 汤姆：这儿是北京时代广场，这是那个公交车站，我们在这儿，明白了吗？

玛丽：明白了，我怎么去梦想大厦？

汤姆：你可以坐出租车去那儿。告诉司机你的目的地，他会带你去那儿。

4. 玛丽：现在提倡低碳出行，我还是坐公交车或地铁吧！最近的地铁站在哪儿？

汤姆：最近的地铁站在建外 SoHo 的角上，挨着图书馆。

5. 玛丽：我怎么去地铁站？

汤姆:你可以坐 40 路公交车,就在那,在 CBD 站下车,你就可以找到地铁站的入口了。

玛丽:然后呢?

汤姆:梦想大厦在古城站附近,所以你先坐地铁 2 号线到崇文门站下,然后转乘 5 号线到古城站下,出站后就可以看到梦想大厦在你的右手边。

6. 玛丽:好的,谢谢您的帮助。

汤姆:不客气。

Situation 5:In a Taxi 在出租车上

1. Taxi Driver:Where are you going?

2. Peter:I'd like to go to Tianhe Airport. What's the flag-fall/flag-down charge?

3. Taxi Driver:It's 10 yuan for the first 3 kilometers and 1.8 yuan per kilometer after that.

4. Peter:I have a flight in 2 hours. How long will it take to get there?

5. Taxi Driver:Don't worry. It only takes about 1 hour.

(40 minutes later)

6. Taxi Driver:Is it a domestic flight or an international flight?

7. Peter:It's an international one.

8. Taxi Driver:That's Terminal 3. Here we are.

9. Peter:How much do I owe you?

10. Taxi Driver:That'll be 78 yuan.

11. Peter:Here is 80 yuan. Keep the change.

12. Taxi Driver:Thanks. Have a good day.

1. 出租车司机:您去哪儿?

2. 彼得:我要去天河机场。起步价是多少?

3. 出租车司机:10 块钱 3 公里。然后每公里 1.8 元。

4. 彼得:我的飞机 2 小时后起飞。到机场要多久?

5. 出租车司机:不用担心,1 小时左右就到了。

(40 分钟后)

6. 出租车司机:您是乘坐国内航班还是国际航班?

7. 彼得:国际航班。

8. 出租车司机:那就是3号航站楼。就是这里了。

9. 彼得:多少钱?

10. 出租车司机:78元。

11. 彼得:给你80元,不用找了。

12. 出租车司机:谢谢!祝您今天愉快。

Situation 6:At the Railway Station 在火车站

Dialogue 1—Buying a ticket 买票

1. Henry:I'd like to buy a ticket to Beijing.

2. Train Conductor:One way or round trip?

3. Henry:One way, please.

4. Train Conductor:Seat or sleeper?

5. Henry:I'd like a hard seat by the window.

6. Train Conductor:When would you like to leave?

7. Henry:October 1st.

8. Train Conductor:I am sorry; there aren't any hard seat tickets available for that day. How about the sleeper?

9. Henry:How much is the fare?

10. Train Conductor:It is 220 yuan for the upper berth, 225 yuan for the middle berth and 230 yuan for the lower berth.

11. Henry:I will have one lower berth ticket.

1. 亨利:我想买一张到北京的票。

2. 火车售票员:单程票还是往返票?

3. 亨利:单程票,谢谢!

4. 火车售票员:硬座还是卧铺?

5. 亨利:我想要一张靠窗的硬座票。

6. 火车售票员:您需要什么时候出发的票?

7. 亨利:十月一号。

8. 火车售票员:对不起,那天的硬座票都卖完了。卧铺票怎么样?

9. 亨利:卧铺票多少钱?

10. 火车售票员:上铺220元,中铺225元,下铺230元。

11. 亨利:我要一张下铺票。

Dialogue 2—Checking in 检票进站

1. Mr White:Shall we check in now?

2. Mrs White:Yes,let's get on board now to avoid the last minute rush.

3. Mr White:We get on board from Platform 3.

4. Mrs White:Oh,here's the ticket-counter. Let's get the tickets punched.

5. Mr White:The train is not in yet.

6. Mrs White:Yes,it is. Look! Our train is on this side.

1. 怀特先生:我们现在可以检票进站吗?

2. 怀特夫人:好的,我们现在上车以免到最后时刻忙乱。

3. 怀特先生:我们要从3站台上车。

4. 怀特夫人:哦,这是检票口,我们去检票吧。

5. 怀特先生:火车还没来。

6. 怀特夫人:来了,你看! 火车就在这边。

Dialogue 3—Luggage Check-in 行李托运

1. Penny:I'd like to check in some luggage.

2. Staff:How many bags?

3. Penny:Three.

4. Staff:Please show me your ticket and ID.

5. Penny:Here you are.

6. Staff:Please fill out this form... This is your luggage claim tag.

7. Penny:OK. When and where can I claim the luggage?

8. Staff:At the luggage claim office after you get off the train.

9. Penny:OK,thank you. Anything else?

10. Staff:Please go over there to weigh the luggage.

1. 潘妮:我想要托运一些行李。

2. 工作人员:一共几个包?

3. 潘妮:3个。
4. 工作人员:请出示你的车票和身份证。
5. 潘妮:给你。
6. 工作人员:请填写这张表格。这是你的行李牌。
7. 潘妮:好的。什么时候在哪可以领取行李?
8. 工作人员:下车后在行李认领办公室领取。
9. 潘妮:好的,谢谢。还有其他事吗?
10. 工作人员:请去那边称行李。

Situation 7:Asking & Giving Directions 问路与指路

Dialogue 1

1. Andy:Can you tell me the way to the station?
2. Ben:Go down this avenue and turn left at the traffic lights.

1. 安迪:请你告诉我去火车站怎么走?
2. 本:沿这条大道一直向前走,在红绿灯那儿向左转。

Dialogue 2

1. Jim:Could you tell me how I can get to the museum?
2. Cathy:Take the No.46 bus,and get off at the square. It's just in front of you.

1. 吉姆:请你告诉我去博物馆怎么走?
2. 凯茜:坐46路公共汽车,在广场下车。它就在你面前。

Dialogue 3

1. Eric:Would you please tell me if there is a hospital nearby?
2. Jane:There is,it's on the corner of Huaihai Street and Xizang Road.

1. 埃里克:请问附近有医院吗?
2. 简:在淮海路和西藏路的路口。

Dialogue 4

1. Eric: Excuse me, where's the men's (ladies') room, please?
2. Jane: Go this way about 5 minutes. When you come to a lane, turn right.

1. 埃里克:请问男(女)洗手间在什么地方?
2. 简:沿着这条路大约走5分钟。当你走到一条小巷时,然后向右拐。

Dialogue 5

1. Jim: Excuse me, how can I get to the No. 1 Middle School?
2. Cathy: Go straight, and then turn right at the second crossing. It is opposite the CBC bank.

1. 吉姆:请问去一中怎么走?
2. 凯茜:直走,在第二个十字路口向右拐。它就在建设银行的对面。

Dialogue 6

1. Peter: Excuse me, where am I on this map?
2. Jessie: We are here at the bus station; we are in the heart of the city.
3. Peter: Oh! I think I'm lost. Can I go from here to the railway station?
4. Jessie: Head straight up the street about two blocks then turn left. It's beside the Holiday Inn.

1. 彼得:对不起,请问我在地图上的什么地方?
2. 杰西:我们在这里,汽车站,我们现在在市中心。
3. 彼得:哦!我想我迷路了。我能否从这里到火车站呢?
4. 杰西:顺着这条街一直走过两个街区,然后左转。它就在假日酒店的旁边。

Dialogue 7

1. Peter: Excuse me, I'm afraid I'm lost. Can you show me the way to the station?
2. Jessie: I'm walking that way. You can follow me and I will show you the way.

1. 彼得:打扰一下,我迷路了,请问您能告诉我去车站怎么走吗?

2. 杰西:我正朝那边去。让我给你带路吧!

Dialogue 8

1. Peter:Excuse me, I wonder if you could help me. I'm looking for the museum.

2. Jessie:Boy, you are lost. It's on the other side of town.

3. Peter:Oh! What bad luck! How can I get to the museum?

4. Jessie:You can take a No. 24 bus here and then transfer to a No. 53 bus to get there.

1. 彼得:打扰一下,不知您能否帮助我,我在找博物馆。

2. 杰西:你是迷路了。它在城的那头。

3. 彼得:啊,太糟糕了!那我怎么去博物馆呢?

4. 杰西:您可以在此乘坐24路公共汽车再换乘53路公共汽车到那里。

Ⅴ. Traveling 旅行篇

The following situational dialogues are all about tourism which concerns losing luggage, packing for a trip, sightseeing, asking someone to take a picture, talking about weather, interview for visa application, and dialogues at the travel agency, in a duty-free shop and at customs.

旅行篇为我们在旅行中所遇场景和进行一系列活动包括在旅行社、免税店、海关、行李遗失、旅行准备、观光、拍照、谈论天气、签证提供了鲜活的情景对话。在口语练习过程中,学生们可采取对话练习、表演等方式熟练掌握并灵活运用以下对话内容。应注意发音准确,语调自然。

Situation 1: At the Travel Agency 在旅行社

Dialogue 1

1. Travel Agent: Good morning. Can I help you?
2. Green: Good morning, I'd like to create a travel itinerary.
3. Travel Agent: Where do you want to go?
4. Green: I have no idea. But I hope to go to the seaside.
5. Travel Agent: Sure, how about Qingdao? It's the best time of the year to visit Qingdao now.
6. Green: I've been there before. I think a southern city would be better.
7. Travel Agent: How about Sanya? Blue sea, soft sand and gentle breezes. It's really relaxing.
8. Green: Sounds great. Do you have any brochures?

1. 旅行代办员:早上好。有什么我可以帮你的吗?
2. 格林:早上好。我想做个旅行计划。
3. 旅行代办员:你想去哪?
4. 格林:不知道。但我希望去海边。
5. 旅行代办员:好的,青岛怎么样? 现在是一年中去青岛的最佳时间。

6. 格林：我去过那儿了。这次最好是去南部城市。

7. 旅行代办员：三亚怎么样？蔚蓝的大海，柔软的沙滩，微风轻轻吹拂。真的很不错。

8. 格林：听起来不错。你有宣传册吗？

Dialogue 2

1. Travel Agent: Welcome, sir. May I help you?

2. Lant: Yes, I want to go to America for my vacation.

3. Travel Agent: No problem. Actually, we have some great packages. It is the most exciting season for Hawaii now. How about a relaxing vacation in Hawaii?

4. Lant: Sounds good. Are there any group tours I can go with?

5. Travel Agent: Yes, there will be one at the end of the month. For many people, a Hawaiian vacation promises languid days filled with sunbathing and poolside cocktails.

6. Lant: Great! I'll take it.

1. 旅行代办员：先生，欢迎光临。我有什么可以帮您的吗？

2. 兰特：我想去美国度假。

3. 旅行代办员：没问题。事实上，我们有一些很棒的套餐。现在是去夏威夷玩最刺激的季节。去夏威夷过一个轻松的假期怎么样？

4. 兰特：听起来不错。有什么旅行团我可以参加吗？

5. 旅行代办员：是的，这个月底会有一个。对很多人来说，一次夏威夷旅行可以带来一段充满日光浴和池边鸡尾酒的慵懒日子。

6. 兰特：太棒了！就它了。

Dialogue 3

1. Travel Agent: Freedom Travel. How may I help you?

2. Anderson: Yes, I'd like to make a flight reservation for the twenty-third of the month.

3. Travel Agent: OK. What is your destination?

4. Anderson: Well. I'm flying to Helsinki in Finland.

5. Travel Agent: OK. Let me check what flights are available... And when do you want to return?

6. Anderson: Uh, well, I'd like to catch a return flight on the twenty-ninth.

7. Travel Agent:OK,could I have your name please?

1. 旅行代办员:自由行。有什么可以帮你吗?
2. 安德森:是的,我想预订这个月23号的航班。
3. 旅行代办员:好的。请问您的目的地是哪?
4. 安德森:我将飞往芬兰的赫尔辛基。
5. 旅行代办员:好的。让我查一下看有哪些航班。您打算什么时候返回?
6. 安德森:噢,我打算29号返回。
7. 旅行代办员:好的。能告诉我您的名字吗?

Dialogue 4

1. Read:Good morning. My wife and I would like to do some sightseeing today. Could you tell us about some places of historical interest in Beijing?
2. Receptionist:My pleasure, sir. Above all, I would recommend the Great Wall. It's amazing.
3. Read:I've heard of it for a long time.
4. Receptionist:Yes. As the saying goes,"He who has never been to the Great Wall is not a true man."
5. Read:Great! Mary,let's go right away.

1. 里德:早上好。今天我太太和我想出去逛逛,你能给我们介绍一些北京的名胜古迹吗?
2. 前台接待:很乐意,先生。我极力推荐长城。它太壮观了!
3. 里德:我耳闻已久了。
4. 前台接待:俗话说,"不到长城非好汉"。
5. 里德:太棒了! 玛丽,我们现在就出发。

Situation 2:Losing Luggage 行李遗失

1. Mr Smith:Excuse me,is this all the luggage?
2. Counter Clerk:Yes,I think so.
3. Mr Smith:My luggage seems to be missing.

4. Counter Clerk: Could I see your luggage claim checks and your full name?

5. Mr Smith: Aaron Smith.

6. Counter Clerk: OK. Just a moment and I'll check it out for you.

7. Counter Clerk: (after several minutes) I'm terribly sorry, Mr Smith. Your luggage seems to have been misplaced.

8. Mr Smith: What am I supposed to do?

9. Counter Clerk: Please fill out this Claim Form with your check number. We'll get in touch with the airline and try our best to get them back.

10. Mr Smith: Thank you.

1. 史密斯先生:请问所有的行李都在这儿吗?

2. 柜台职员:对,我想是的。

3. 史密斯先生:我的行李似乎丢失了。

4. 柜台职员:我可以看看您的行李认领单吗? 请问您的全名是?

5. 史密斯先生:我叫艾伦·史密斯。

6. 柜台职员:好的,请稍等。我来为您核查一下。

7. 柜台职员:(几分钟后)史密斯先生,很抱歉,您的行李似乎误放了。

8. 史密斯先生:那我应该怎么做呢?

9. 柜台职员:请把您的行李号码填写在行李遗失申请表中。我们会与航空公司联系,并尽全力找回您的行李。

10. 史密斯先生:谢谢。

Situation 3: Packing for a Trip 旅行准备

1. George: Hello, darling, are you all set? We have to go now.

2. Jane: Not yet, George. I'm still packing up things.

3. George: Darling, why are you taking such a big suitcase? It's only a 4-day trip. Tell me what you put in here.

4. Jane: Our clothes, of course. I was told that it might be cold on the top of the mountain, so I packed our light jackets.

5. George: Why are you taking so much medicine?

6. Jane: Remember you had a diarrhea last time we went to Jiuzhaigou. Thank god I

brought Imodium. So I have a bit of this and a bit of that just in case.

7. George: But darling, why are you taking a mini fan?

8. Jane: It's very hot there. At least I can have some air wherever I go.

9. George: Anyway, we need to leave or we will be late.

10. Jane: Wait a minute. I forgot the sunblock and the hiking backpack. We'll definitely need them.

11. George: Darling, I am begging you. We've got to go now. We can buy things in the local areas, right?

12. Jane: OK. Off we go. George!

1. 乔治:嗨! 亲爱的,你都准备好了吗? 我们得出发了。

2. 简:还没有呢,乔治。我还在打包行李。

3. 乔治:亲爱的,你为什么要带这么大一个箱子呢? 这只是四天的旅行呀! 告诉我你都带了些什么?

4. 简:当然是我们的衣服啦。我听说山顶上可能会有点儿冷,所以我把我们的薄夹克带了。

5. 乔治:为什么要带这么多药呢?

6. 简:还记得上次去九寨沟的时候,你腹泻吗? 幸亏当时我带了泻立停。所以以防万一,各种药我都带了一点儿。

7. 乔治:但是亲爱的,为什么你要带上这个小风扇呢?

8. 简:那儿非常热。这样我走到哪,哪都有风。

9. 乔治:不管怎样,我们得出发了,不然就迟到了。

10. 简:等会儿,我忘带防晒霜和登山包了,我们绝对会需要它们的。

11. 乔治:亲爱的,求求你了,我们必须走啦。我们也可以在当地买东西的,对吧?

12. 简:好! 乔治,我们走吧!

Situation 4:In a Duty-free Shop 在免税店

1. Jane: Is this a duty-free shop?

2. Salesgirl: Yes, lady. What can I do for you?

3. Jane: I want to buy some specialties. Can you recommend something?

4. Salesgirl: Sure. I strongly advise you buy a bottle of perfume and a lighter.

5. Jane: Fine. They look nice. I will take both of them. And may I have the bill, please?

6. Salesgirl: It comes to $100.

7. Jane: Can I pay with a personal check?

8. Salesgirl: Sure. Here is your receipt and you can reclaim the tax paid on these goods at customs.

9. Jane: Could you please tell me how I can draw my tax?

10. Salesgirl: Yes. Here is the tax-refund form, and you should fill it out according to the requirement. You can bring it together with your receipt, articles, boarding pass and passport to the customs, and show them to the officers. You can get 10 dollars back.

11. Jane: Thanks a lot.

12. Salesgirl: Not at all.

1. 简:这里是免税商店吗?

2. 女售货员:是的,我能帮您忙吗?

3. 简:我想买些特产,你能给我推荐些吗?

4. 女售货员:好的,我强烈建议您买一瓶香水和一个打火机。

5. 简:看上去不错,我两个都要了。我想结账。

6. 女售货员:总共是100美元。

7. 简:我能用私人支票付账吗?

8. 女售货员:当然可以,这是发票,您可以在海关办理退税。

9. 简:请问你能告诉我如何办理退税吗?

10. 女售货员:好的。这是你的退税表格,你按要求填写个人信息。然后去海关,向海关人员出示你的发票、购买的商品、登机牌以及护照。您能得到10美元的退税款。

11. 简:非常感谢。

12. 女售货员:不用谢。

Situation 5: Sightseeing 观光

1. Tour Guide: We are now in Paris, France. This is the park called Champ de Mars. It is near the Seine River. Do you see the tower in front of us? That's the famous Eiffel Tower. It was built by a famous engineer Gustave Eiffel in 1889 for the World's Fair.

2. Jane: How tall is it?

3. Tour Guide: It is 320 meters high and kept the record as the tallest structure in the world until 1930.

4. Jane: All these buildings are really magnificent. This journey is well worthwhile. How many travelers come here every year?

5. Tour Guide: Yes. Millions of travelers come here every year to see these buildings.

6. Tour Guide: OK. Now let's go to visit the Louvre as scheduled.

1. 导游：我们现在位于法国巴黎,塞纳河畔的战神广场。看到我们前方的塔了吗？那就是著名的埃菲尔铁塔。它是为1889年的世界博览会而特意建造的。它的建造者是著名的工程师古斯塔夫·埃菲尔。

2. 简：这建筑有多高呢？

3. 导游：有320米高,在1930年前一直是世界第一高建筑。

4. 简：这座建筑太宏伟了。这趟旅行很值得。每年有多少游客来这儿？

5. 导游：是的,每年都有百万游客来这里参观这座建筑。

6. 导游：好,接下来让我们按计划去参观卢浮宫吧。

Situation 6: Asking Someone to Take a Picture 请人拍照

1. Jane: Excuse me. Would you mind taking a picture for us?

2. Tom: Of course not, but I'm afraid I don't know how to use your camera.

3. Jane: It's simple, just press the button. Like this.

4. Tom: I see. Which background would you like, the landscape or the landmark?

5. Jane: We prefer the landmark because it is meaningful and typical.

6. Tom: OK. I will focus on the landmark. Hold your position and say cheese.

7. Jane: Oh, this group photo looks great! You are such a professional photographer. Could you please take another individual photo for me?

8. Tom: Sure, it's my pleasure!

1. 简：打扰一下,你介意为我们拍张照吗？

2. 汤姆：当然不介意了。但我恐怕不会用你的相机。

3. 简：很简单,按这个按钮就可以了,像这样。

4. 汤姆：我明白了。你们喜欢哪个背景？风景还是地标？

5. 简:我们更喜欢地标,因为它很有意义而且具有代表性。

6. 汤姆:好的,我会把镜头聚焦到地标上。请你们保持姿势说"茄子"。

7. 简:噢! 这张合影拍得太棒了! 你简直是专业级的摄影师。你能再帮我拍张单人照吗?

8. 汤姆:当然可以,乐意效劳。

Situation 7:Talking about Weather 谈论天气

Dialogue 1

1. Jane:Is there a lot of snow in Toronto at this time of the year?

2. David:Yes. The snow is so heavy here.

3. Jane:Well. I think I like it. I like snow very much.

4. David:Yes. It's really so beautiful with everything covered by snow.

5. Jane:By the way,where can I go skiing?

6. David:There is a ski resort around. You can take Bus 12 and get off at the last stop.

7. Jane:Thanks a lot.

8. David:Not at all.

1. 简:多伦多每年这个时候经常下雪吗?

2. 大卫:是的,经常有暴雪。

3. 简:我很喜欢这样,我非常喜欢雪。

4. 大卫:的确,万物在大雪覆盖下显得非常好看。

5. 简:顺便问一下,哪里可以滑雪?

6. 大卫:附近有个滑雪场。你可以乘坐12路车到终点站下车。

7. 简:非常感谢。

8. 大卫:不用谢。

Dialogue 2

1. David:You don't look very well. Do you have a cold?

2. Jane:Yes,I'm not feeling very well. I think I've got a bad cold.

3. David:Is it because of the bad weather in the past few days?

4. Jane: Hasn't it! It's been cold and windy recently. Do you like the weather here?

5. David: Not really, but I've got used to it now. So do you have any traveling plans?

6. Jane: Oh, yes. I'm going to New York for a trip this autumn. What's the weather like in New York?

7. David: Not so good. It's windy and dry. We've got a continental climate there. It's dry all the year round. Usually autumn is the best season of the year in New York.

8. Jane: Is it cold there in autumn? Should I take any warm clothes with me?

9. David: No, it isn't very cold at that time. You'll only need some light wool clothing with some jackets and shirts.

1. 大卫：你的脸色不太好。你感冒了吗？

2. 简：我觉得不太舒服，我想我是感冒了。

3. 大卫：你是因为天气不好病了吗？

4. 简：可不是嘛！最近很冷，风又大。你喜欢这儿的天气吗？

5. 大卫：不太喜欢，但是我已经习惯了。

6. 简：噢，我秋天要到纽约去游玩，那儿的天气怎么样？

7. 大卫：天气不是很好，风多又干燥。那里是大陆性气候，终年干燥。秋天通常是纽约一年中最好的季节。

8. 简：那儿的秋天很冷吗？我需要带很多保暖衣服吗？

9. 大卫：不用，那时不会太冷。你只需带些薄毛衣，加上几件外套和衬衣就行了。

Situation 8: At Customs 在海关

1. Customs Officer: Good morning, sir. May I see your passport?

2. George: Sure, here you are.

3. Customs Officer: Thank you. Is this your luggage?

4. George: No, some of it is my mother's. Do you want her passport, too?

5. Customs Officer: Yes, please. Do you have any personal luggage?

6. George: Yes. Do you want those on the belt, too?

7. Customs Officer: Yes, please.

8. Customs Officer: Would you please open this big suitcase?

9. George: Sure. There are just some clothes and toiletries in it.

10. Customs Officer: I see. Do you have anything to declare? Tobacco or alcohol?

11. George: No, we don't have such things.

12. Customs Officer: Any prohibited articles? Any fresh food, live plants, or animals?

13. George: Oh, no ma'am, none of that.

14. Customs Officer: Thank you. You may lock up your suitcase. Here are your passports.

15. George: Thanks a lot.

1. 海关官员:先生,早安。我可以看一下你的护照吗?

2. 乔治:当然。护照在这儿。

3. 海关官员:谢谢。这些行李是你的吗?

4. 乔治:不,有一些是我妈妈的。你也要看她的护照吗?

5. 海关官员:是的,麻烦一下。你们有没有随身行李呢?

6. 乔治:有。随身行李也要放上输送带吗?

7. 海关官员:是的,麻烦你了。

8. 海关官员:可否请你打开这个大行李箱?

9. 乔治:当然。里面只有一些衣服和盥洗用品。

10. 海关官员:你们有没有要报税的物品呢? 比如烟酒类。

11. 乔治:没有,我们没有带任何烟酒。

12. 海关官员:有没有任何违禁品? 有没有新鲜食品、植物或动物?

13. 乔治:哦,没有,女士。都没有。

14. 海关官员:谢谢。你可以将行李锁上了。护照还给你们。

15. 乔治:非常感谢你。

Situation 9: Interview for Visa Application 签证面谈

1. Interviewer: Hi. I am the interviewer today. Do you take what we need for your visa application?

2. Tom: OK. Here is my application form and all the documents.

3. Interviewer: Can you tell me why you want a visa to America?

4. Tom: Because I want to have a view of the exotic landscapes in order to extend my horizon and get to know the world better.

5. Interviewer: OK. Do you plan to go to America on your own or with your family?
6. Tom: By myself.
7. Interviewer: Are you ready to go now?
8. Tom: Yes, I'm ready.

1. 面试官:你好。今天我负责对你的签证申请进行面试。你带了相关材料吗?
2. 汤姆:好的,这是我的申请表和申请资料。
3. 面试官:能告诉我你为什么想要申请美国的签证吗?
4. 汤姆:因为我一直想要领略一下异域风光,以开阔自己的视野,增进对世界的了解。
5. 面试官:好的,你打算自己去还是和家人一起去呢?
6. 汤姆:我打算一个人去。
7. 面试官:那你对你的行程都准备好了吗?
8. 汤姆:是的,都准备好了。

Ⅵ. Catering 餐饮篇

Good service in fluent English helps your customers to enjoy their meals, brings your restaurant a good reputation and makes your restaurant more attractive to customers. This chapter teaches you oral English in food and restaurant situations, including: introduction to restaurants, recommendation of dishes, and how to help your customers, etc.

流畅的英文服务不仅能让客人愉快地用餐,还能为你的餐厅带来好口碑,吸引更多的客人。餐饮篇能帮助你学到餐厅服务必备的英语口语,包括介绍餐厅、推荐菜肴、服务客人,等等。

Dialogue 1

1. Peter: Excuse me, can you suggest a good restaurant?
2. Tom: Yes. What kind of food would you like to eat?
3. Peter: Are there any Chinese restaurants around here?
4. Tom: There's one across the street.
5. Peter: Where can I find the best local food?
6. Tom: I suggest you try Green Inn.
7. Peter: Is it very far from here?

1. 彼得:请问,你能推荐一家好的餐厅吗?
2. 汤姆:好的,你想吃什么样的东西?
3. 彼得:这附近有没有中国餐厅?
4. 汤姆:对街有一家。
5. 彼得:哪里可吃到最好的本地食物?
6. 汤姆:我建议你去格林餐厅试试看。
7. 彼得:离这里很远吗?

Dialogue 2

1. Bill: This way, please. This is your table.
2. Jack: Well, can I have that table by the window? We want to enjoy the night view of New York.

3. Bill: How about this table, sir?

4. Jack: This is just fine, thank you.

1. 比尔：请这边走，这是你的桌位。

2. 杰克：嗯，我们可以坐靠窗的位子吗？我们想欣赏一下纽约的夜景。

3. 比尔：先生，这个桌位如何？

4. 杰克：好的，谢谢。

Dialogue 3

1. William: Good morning. May I take your order now?

2. Jim: Please give me a few minutes. I'm not yet ready.

3. William: Please take your time.

4. Jim: Waiter... I'd like to have a full breakfast.

5. William: Certainly, sir. Which kind of juice would you like?

6. Jim: Orange.

7. William: Would you like sausage, bacon or ham?

8. Jim: Sausage, please.

9. William: How would you like your eggs, sir?

10. Jim: Two fried eggs, over easy.

11. William: Certainly. Would you like toast, breakfast rolls, croissants or Danish pastries?

12. Jim: Croissants, please. And I'd like to have a black tea.

13. William: Certainly, sir. So that's orange juice, sausage and two eggs, over easy, croissant and a black tea.

14. Jim: That's right.

15. William: Thank you, sir.

1. 威廉：早上好，您现在点餐吗？

2. 吉姆：再给我几分钟，我还没有准备好。

3. 威廉：请慢慢挑选，先生。

4. 吉姆：服务员……我想要全英式早餐。

5. 威廉：好的，先生，你要什么果汁？

6. 吉姆：橙汁。

7. 威廉：您要香肠、培根还是火腿？

8. 吉姆：香肠。

9. 威廉：您喜欢鸡蛋怎么做？

10. 吉姆：两个鸡蛋，两面煎。

11. 威廉：好的，您喜欢吐司面包、早餐软包、牛角包还是丹麦包？

12. 吉姆：牛角包。我还要红茶。

13. 威廉：好的，先生。您点了橙汁、香肠、两面煎的煎蛋、牛角包和一杯红茶。

14. 吉姆：对的。

15. 威廉：谢谢，先生。

Dialogue 4

1. David: Welcome to Parklane Restaurant. How many people are there in your party?

2. Sam: Three.

3. David: Would you like your table in the smoking area or non-smoking area?

4. Sam: Smoking.

5. David: Follow me, please. I'll seat you. How about this table?

6. Sam: Yes. Thank you.

7. David: Please take a seat. Here's the menu. Take your time please. I'll take your order in a moment. Would you like something to drink first?

8. Sam: We have three Tsingtao beers.

9. David: Just a moment. I'll bring them for you right away.

1. 大卫：欢迎来到柏宁餐厅。请问总共有几位呢？

2. 山姆：三位。

3. 大卫：您喜欢坐吸烟区还是无烟区呢？

4. 山姆：吸烟区。

5. 大卫：请跟我来。我给您找位子。这张桌子可以吗？

6. 山姆：好的。谢谢。

7. 大卫：请坐。这是菜单。请慢慢看。稍后我来帮您点单。先来点喝的怎么样？

8. 山姆：给我们来三支青岛啤酒。

9. 大卫：请稍等。我马上去拿过来。

Dialogue 5

1. Betty: Good evening, gentlemen. Have you made a reservation?
2. Alan: No. I'm afraid we haven't.
3. Betty: Never mind, sir. A table for two? This way, please.
4. Alan: Can we sit here by the window?
5. Betty: I'm sorry, sir. That table has been reserved. There is a sign on it. I'll seat you at another table.
6. Alan: OK, thanks.
7. Betty: Would you like to have a drink first?
8. Alan: Yes. We'll have two beers.
9. Betty: Two beers. Certainly, sir.
10. Alan: Can we have the menu please?
11. Betty: Here's the menu, sir. I'll be back to take your order in a minute.

1. 贝蒂:先生们,晚上好,请问您有预定吗?
2. 艾伦:恐怕没有。
3. 贝蒂:没关系,先生。是两位吗?请这边走。
4. 艾伦:我们可以坐到靠窗的位子吗?
5. 贝蒂:不好意思,先生,这个位已被预定了,这里有预定的标志。我给您找另一张桌子吧。
6. 艾伦:好的,谢谢。
7. 贝蒂:先来点喝的怎么样?
8. 艾伦:好的,先来两杯啤酒吧。
9. 贝蒂:好的。先生。
10. 艾伦:请拿菜单给我们。
11. 贝蒂:菜单在这里,先生。我稍后再来为您点菜下单。

Ⅶ. Entertainment & Culture 娱乐和文化篇

The following situational dialogues are about entertainment and culture. People's social life at the cinema, museum, concert and theatre are presented.

娱乐和文化篇的情景对话的场景主要在影院、博物馆、音乐会和剧院。

在口语练习过程中,学生们可采取对话练习、表演等方式进行学习。应注意发音准确,语调自然。请看下面的情景对话:

Situation 1: At the Cinema 在电影院

Dialogue 1

1. John: Hi, I'd like two tickets for *Avatar* please.
2. Susan: Would you prefer to sit in the front, middle or at the back?
3. John: The back please. Oh, and do you offer a student discount?
4. Susan: Yes, we do. Are you both students?
5. John: Yes, here are our student cards.
6. Susan: OK, that'll be $18 please.
7. John: Here you are.
8. Susan: Thanks, here are your tickets, you need to go to Cinema Five.
9. John: Thank you very much.

(They then go to get some snacks.)

10. John: Hello, I'd like medium popcorn and a small coke please.
11. Carol: OK, coming up... That's $7 please.
12. John: Here you are.
13. Carol: Thanks. Enjoy your film.

1. 约翰:您好,买两张《阿凡达》电影票。
2. 苏珊:您喜欢前排、中间还是靠后的位置?
3. 约翰:后排吧。你们给学生提供折扣吗?
4. 苏珊:是的,你俩都是学生吗?

5. 约翰:是的,这是我们的学生卡。
6. 苏珊:好的,一共18美元。
7. 约翰:给您。
8. 苏珊:谢谢,这是你们的电影票,你们要去5号厅。
9. 约翰:非常感谢。

(接着他们去买零食。)

10. 约翰:您好,请来份中号玉米花和小杯可乐。
11. 卡罗:来啦。7美元,谢谢。
12. 约翰:给您。
13. 卡罗:谢谢,请欣赏电影。

Dialogue 2

1. John:The movie is about to start. Let's hurry.
2. Susan:Wait a moment. I'm going to buy some snacks.
3. John:Then be quick.
4. Susan:What would you like?
5. John:Popcorn and cola.
6. Susan:OK,I'll be right back.

1. 约翰:电影快开始了。我们赶紧吧。
2. 苏珊:等一下。我去买点儿零食。
3. 约翰:那你快点儿。
4. 苏珊:你要吃什么?
5. 约翰:爆米花和可乐。
6. 苏珊:好的,马上回来。

Dialogue 3

1. John:OK. Susan,let's talk about movies.
2. Susan:OK,great! I'm a big movie fan.
3. John:What is your favorite type of movie? Romance,action,or suspense?
4. Susan:I love science fiction.

1. 约翰:苏珊,我们来聊聊电影。

2. 苏珊:好的,太棒了! 我是个电影迷。

3. 约翰:你喜欢哪种类型的电影? 爱情片、动作片,还是悬疑片?

4. 苏珊:我喜欢的是科幻片。

Situation 2:At the Shanghai World Expo 在上海世博会

Steven and May pay a visit to the China Pavilion of the Shanghai World Exposition, and they see some fantastic exhibits.

史蒂文和梅一起去参观上海世博会中国馆,他们看到了很多精美的展品。

1. Steven:May,is this the China Pavilion of the Shanghai World Exposition?

May:Yes.

2. Steven:How magnificent it is! It's a red building. Why is it red?

May:Because red symbolizes joyfulness and happiness in Chinese culture. Red is the color of luck.

(after entering the China Pavilion)

3. Steven:How cute the doll is!

May:It's the mascot of the Shanghai World Expo. It's called Haibao.

4. Steven:And it's made of china. How exquisite it is!

May:Absolutely.

5. Steven:There are some delicate vases,artifacts,splendid paintings and photography works over there. Let's go and have a look.

May:That's fantastic! What a rewarding experience it is!

1. 史蒂文:梅,这是上海世博会中国馆吗?

梅:是啊。

2. 史蒂文:好壮观啊! 它是一栋红色的建筑,为什么是红色呢?

梅:因为红色在中国文化里象征着喜庆吉祥,红色是一种吉利的颜色。

(进入中国馆后)

3. 史蒂文:这个娃娃好可爱啊!

梅:它是上海世博会的吉祥物,它的名字叫海宝。

4. 史蒂文:而且它是用瓷器做的。好精致啊!

梅:是啊!

5. 史蒂文:那边还有精美的花瓶、工艺品、绘画和摄影作品。我们过去看看吧!

梅:太漂亮了! 今天真是大开眼界啊!

Situation 3:At the Museum 在博物馆

Steven and May pay a visit to the museum of historic relics, and they see some precious things.

史蒂文和梅一起去参观历史文物博物馆,看到了很多珍贵的东西。

1. Steven:May,is this the Hall of Ancient China?
2. May:Yes. Look at these historical relics,amazing!
3. Steven:Why are they all in glass boxes?
4. May:For protection. Some relics will turn to dust if exposed to air.
5. Steven:So there isn't air in the glass boxes?
6. May:No,there isn't. Every box is vacuum sealed.
7. Steven:I wonder how old these things are. Thousands of years?
8. May:Yeah,they all come from a very ancient time.
9. Steven:Hey,look at that tripod. I've seen it on TV.
10. May:It was made 4000 years ago. It's priceless!

1. 史蒂文:梅,这是古代中国馆吗?
2. 梅:是啊。看这些文物,真令人惊叹!
3. 史蒂文:为什么它们都被装在玻璃箱里呢?
4. 梅:为了保护它们啊。一些文物暴露在空气中就会变成粉末。
5. 史蒂文:那玻璃箱中就没有空气了?
6. 梅:没有。它们都是真空的。
7. 史蒂文:真不知这些东西有多古老,几千年?
8. 梅:是啊,它们都是来自古代。
9. 史蒂文:嘿,看这个鼎。我在电视上看到过。
10. 梅:4000 年前的鼎。这可是无价之宝!

Situation 4: At the Concert 在音乐厅

Dialogue 1

1. Steven: I will go to a concert tomorrow.

2. May: Concert?

3. Steven: Yes, it's a violin concert. Would you like to join me?

4. May: Sure. I'd love to.

5. Steven: Do you like classical music?

6. May: Yes. My hobby is listening to classical music.

7. Steven: Cool! I love it, too. Let's go together tomorrow.

8. May: OK. I can't wait.

9. Steven: Me too.

1. 史蒂文:我明天要去听音乐会。

2. 梅:音乐会?

3. 史蒂文:是的,是一个小提琴演奏会。你要和我一起去吗?

4. 梅:好啊。我很喜欢。

5. 史蒂文:你喜欢古典音乐吗?

6. 梅:是的。我的爱好是听古典音乐。

7. 史蒂文:酷! 我也喜欢它。我们明天一起去看。

8. 梅:好的。我都等不及了。

9. 史蒂文:我也是。

Dialogue 2

1. Steven: I am going to a concert tonight.

2. May: Do you know which band is performing?

3. Steven: A famous band from Germany.

4. May: I love listening to live music, it's so beautiful!

5. Steven: It is very different from listening to CDs.

6. May: Of course. It's more enjoyable to be at a concert.

7. Steven: The sound leaves you with lasting memories.

8. May: Yes, it's compelling!

1. 史蒂文:今晚我要去音乐会。

2. 梅:你知道是哪个乐团演奏吗?

3. 史蒂文:它是由德国一个著名的乐团演奏的。

4. 梅:我喜欢听现场演奏的音乐,非常动听!

5. 史蒂文:这和听CD很不一样。

6. 梅:当然。听音乐会更是一种享受。

7. 史蒂文:这种声音让人回味无穷。

8. 梅:是的,太震撼了!

Dialogue 3

1. Steven: Would you like to stretch your legs?

2. May: Sure.

3. Steven: Let's get a soft drink.

4. May: Do we have enough time?

5. Steven: It's a fifteen-minute intermission.

6. May: The seats are excellent. We're right in the center.

7. Steven: It's a new concert hall and the acoustics is great.

8. May: I couldn't agree with you more.

9. Steven: Is this your first time to come to a symphony concert?

10. May: In the United States, yes. But back in China, I went to concerts a couple of times with my parents.

11. Steven: Are there large concert halls in your city?

12. May: We have two. One is like this one. The other is a little smaller.

13. Steven: That's great. Well, we'd better get back to our seats. It's about to start.

1. 史蒂文:你愿意起来活动活动吗?

2. 梅:好啊。

3. 史蒂文:咱们去喝点饮料吧。

4. 梅:时间够吗?

5. 史蒂文:中场休息15分钟。

6. 梅:位子好极了。咱们刚好在正当中。

7. 史蒂文:这是个新建的音乐厅,音响效果特别好。

8. 梅:完全同意。

9. 史蒂文:你是第一次到音乐厅来听交响乐吗?

10. 梅:在美国是第一次。不过在中国时我和父母去听过几次音乐会。

11. 史蒂文:你们那个城市有大音乐厅吗?

12. 梅:有两个,有一个和这个差不多,另一个稍微小一点。

13. 史蒂文:那好极了。咱们得回到座位上去,差不多又要开始了。

Situation 5:At a Fashion Show 在时装秀

Dialogue 1

1. Sophie:Look at these clothes designed by the top fashion designers. What do you think of them?

2. May:Well, they look lovely, but for me, they are impractical. I mean, would you wear such clothes to your office or walking down the street?

3. Sophie:I got what you meant. People may think you are strange if you wear something like that in daily life.

4. May:Yeah, that's exactly what I think. I am not sure why they have fashion shows like this. I don't think many people would buy these clothes. It seems like a waste of money.

5. Sophie:Well, I couldn't agree with you on that point. Fashion shows give fashion designers an opportunity to show what they would like to see people wearing. Besides, it is a great advertising, since many journalists and photographers are there.

6. May:You are probably right. No wonder many fashion designers are willing to spend a lot of time and money on it.

7. Sophie:Yeah. People spend a lot of money on fashion. They are not necessarily wasting their money. Changes in fashion help to create new technologies and also jobs for people.

8. May:Sounds reasonable. So shall we go shopping this afternoon? It occurs to me

that I need to buy some clothes.

9. Sophie:Great! Let's go shopping.

1. 苏菲:看看顶级时装设计师们设计的这些衣服,你觉得它们怎么样?

2. 梅:看起来挺好看的。但于我而言,它们并不实用。我是说,你会穿这样的衣服去办公室或者是在大街上走吗?

3. 苏菲:懂你的意思。平常生活中穿成这样会让人觉得你很奇怪。

4. 梅:是的,这正是我的看法。我不清楚为什么要举办这样的时装秀。我觉得多数人都不会愿意去买这种时装秀上的衣服。感觉举办时装秀是浪费钱。

5. 苏菲:这一点我不太同意。时装设计师们通过举办时装秀来告诉大家他们希望我们穿什么样的衣服。而且,举办时装秀是很好的宣传渠道,因为现场会有很多记者和摄影师在。

6. 梅:或许如你所说吧。难怪时装设计师们会愿意花很多时间和金钱举办时装秀。

7. 苏菲:是的。人们会花很多钱在流行上,这并不一定都是在浪费钱。流行的变迁带动科技创新,也同样给人们提供就业机会。

8. 梅:是挺有道理的。下午去购物怎么样? 突然想起来,我需要买衣服了。

9. 苏菲:好主意,那一起去购物吧。

Dialogue 2

1. Mary:Hey,what are you doing here?

2. Sophie:Hi! I am reading a fashion magazine.

3. Mary:Interesting! Would you mind reading with me?

4. Sophie:Of course not. Come here and take a seat.

5. Mary:OK.

6. Sophie:I really appreciate the works of some successful fashion designers. Look at the clothes,decoration and hair of these models. Fantastic!

7. Mary: Yes, I agree. Fashion designers are crucial figures of fashion industry and they contribute greatly to it.

8. Sophie:Indeed. To tell you the truth,my dream profession is fashion designer.

9. Mary:Oh,really? That's amazing! But as far as I know,fashion designers' life is never easy, since they are engaged in designing, showing and producing.

10. Sophie: I know. Fashion designers are also under great pressure in this highly

competitive industry. Still, I will try my best to realize my dream.

11. Mary: Good. May your dream come true!

12. Sophie: Thank you!

1. 玛丽：嘿，在干什么呢？

2. 苏菲：在读一本时尚杂志。

3. 玛丽：挺有意思的。介意一起读吗？

4. 苏菲：当然不介意了，过来坐吧！

5. 玛丽：好的。

6. 苏菲：真的挺欣赏那些成功的时装设计师的作品。看看这些模特的衣着、装饰和发型，太棒了！

7. 玛丽：是的，同意你的观点。时装设计师们是时装行业的关键人物，对这个行业贡献很大。

8. 苏菲：确实。说实话，我梦想的职业就是时装设计师。

9. 玛丽：真的吗？很棒！但据我所知，时装设计师的生活并不轻松，因为他们要投身于设计、展示和制作。

10. 苏菲：我知道。在这个高度竞争的行业中，他们还面临很多压力。但我仍然会尽全力去实现这一梦想。

11. 玛丽：挺好的，愿你梦想成真！

12. 苏菲：谢谢！

Ⅷ. Interview 求职面试篇

The following situational dialogues are about job interview questions and answers, like self-introduction, reasons for application, work experience, weaknesses and strengths, achievements and characteristics.

求职面试是每一名学生都将要面临的情境,求职面试篇为我们在求职面试时进行自我介绍、讲述应聘原因、谈论工作经验、评价优缺点和成绩、描述个人性格等提供了鲜活的情境对话,在口语练习过程中学生们可采取对话练习、表演等方式来熟练掌握并灵活运用以下对话内容。应注意在练习和应用过程中发音准确,语调自然。

Situation 1:Self-introduction 自我介绍

(Interviewer 面试官:Mrs Smith

Applicant 应聘者:Mr Wu)

1. Mrs Smith:Would you please briefly introduce yourself to us?
2. Mr Wu:With pleasure. Good morning, everyone. It's a pleasure for me to have this opportunity to present myself to you. My name is Yue Wu, a candidate for the position of sales representative. I come from Wuhan, the capital of Hubei province. I graduated from Wuhan College of Foreign Languages & Foreign Affairs, and majored in marketing. I passed CET4 and 6 with high scores. During those semesters, I was awarded the first-place scholarship. In order to develop in an all round way, I took part in various competitions and relevant activities and benefited a lot from these experiences. In 2015, I took an internship at Wuhan Hotel as an assistant to the manager, working there for 6 months and gaining much experience. I'm an excellent team player and problem-solver. I believe I'm well suited and qualified for this position.

1. 史密斯女士:你能简短地介绍一下自己吗?
2. 吴先生:非常乐意。各位早上好,很高兴有机会在此做自我介绍。我叫吴越,来应聘销售代表。我来自湖北武汉,毕业于武汉外语外事职业学院,主修市场营销。我以优异的成绩通过了英语四、六级考试。在三年学习中,我获得了一等奖学金。为了全面发展,我参加了各种竞赛和活动,受益颇多。2015 年我在武汉酒店实习,在经理助理职位上实习了六个月,学到了很多经验。我具有良好的团队精神和解决问题能力。我相信我定能胜任销售代表这个职位。

Situation 2: About Reason for Application 应聘理由

(Interviewer 面试官:Mrs Smith

Applicant 应聘者:Mr Wu)

Dialogue 1

1. Mr Wu: Excuse me. May I see Mrs. Smith?

2. Mrs Smith: That's me. What can I do for you?

3. Mr Wu: Nice to meet you, Mrs. Smith. I'm here for an interview by appointment.

4. Mrs Smith: Are you Mr. Wu?

5. Mr Wu: Yes, I am.

6. Mrs Smith: Nice to meet you, too. Did you have any difficulty looking for our company?

7. Mr Wu: Not really. I am familiar with this area.

1. 吴先生:劳驾,我可以见史密斯女士吗?

2. 史密斯女士:我就是,需要我帮忙吗?

3. 吴先生:很高兴见到你,史密斯女士。我是应约来面试的。

4. 史密斯女士:你是吴先生吧?

5. 吴先生:是的,我是。

6. 史密斯女士:我也很高兴见到你。找我们公司困难吗?

7. 吴先生:没有,我对这一带很熟悉。

Dialogue 2

1. Mrs Smith: What has made you choose this company?

2. Mr Wu: Your company has had a good reputation not only for your high-quality products, but also for your well-structured management. I'd like to be a part of such an outstanding company which cares not only for the customers' needs, but also for the

welfare of the employees.

3. Mrs Smith: What do you know about our company?

4. Mr Wu: It was established in Shanghai in 1940, it is one of the leading trading companies in China with a total of 40 million US dollars. It employs more than 17,000 staff throughout the world.

5. Mrs Smith: Thank you for your interest in this position. Why do you consider yourself qualified for the job?

6. Mr Wu: I have the educational background and relevant experience required by the job. Besides, I am a very good team player and have a burning desire to succeed.

7. Mrs Smith: What interests you most about this job?

8. Mr Wu: I'd like to work in a team and enjoy helping in solving problems.

9. Mrs Smith: Have you applied for a similar post to any other companies?

10. Mr Wu: Yes, I've applied to General Electric China Incorporation but that was just to get experience in being interviewed. I'm afraid it would be hard for me to get employed by such a large company. That's why I want to work for your company.

11. Mrs Smith: What was the result of your application to that company?

12. Mr Wu: They turned me down.

13. Mrs Smith: Why didn't you get the job?

14. Mr Wu: The reason was that I was too nervous to express myself clearly during the interview.

1. 史密斯女士：你为什么会选择这家公司？

2. 吴先生：贵公司一直享有盛名，不仅因为你们产品质量好，而且有着极其完善的管理系统。我希望能在一家既注重客户需求，又关注员工福利的公司内尽其所能。

3. 史密斯女士：对我们公司，你了解多少？

4. 吴先生：我知道贵公司是当今中国最大的贸易公司之一。它于1940年在上海建立，总资产达4000万美元，且全球雇有超过1.7万名员工。

5. 史密斯女士：谢谢你对本公司的关注，为何你认为自己具有这项职位的资格？

6. 吴先生：我有与此工作有关的教育及工作经验。此外，我是一个很好的团队合作者，并有强烈渴望成功的信念。

7. 史密斯女士：你对这份工作最感兴趣的是什么？

8. 吴先生：我喜欢和一群人一起工作，一起解决问题。

9. 史密斯女士:你有没有向其他公司应聘类似的职位?

10. 吴先生:有,我申请了美国通用电气中国公司,但那只是为了获得面试的经验。对我而言,被一家那样的大公司雇用可能是一件很难的事情,所以我想到贵公司试试。

11. 史密斯女士:你申请那家公司的结果如何?

12. 吴先生:他们拒绝了我。

13. 史密斯女士:你认为自己为什么没有获得那个职位?

14. 吴先生:我想是因为面试时太紧张了,我未能清晰地表达自己的观点。

Dialogue 3

1. Mrs Smith: What's your career objective?

2. Mr Wu: I want to use my knowledge and experience in a large firm.

3. Mrs Smith: What would you like to be five years from now?

4. Mr Wu: I hope I could be the leader of an energetic and productive sales team.

5. Mrs Smith: What do you consider important when looking for a job?

6. Mr Wu: I think the most important thing is the nature of the job. One should never do anything one is not interested in. To me, a pleasant working condition with cooperative staff is also important.

7. Mrs Smith: What do you think you would bring to the job?

8. Mr Wu: My business experience and knowledge in marketing. I know a lot about how the Chinese market works and how business is done. And I am a hard worker when I have something challenging to do.

1. 史密斯女士:你的职业目标是什么?

2. 吴先生:我希望能在一家大企业运用自己所学的知识和经验。

3. 史密斯女士:五年之后你希望从事什么样的工作?

4. 吴先生:我希望能成为一支有活力及高效率的销售队伍的主管。

5. 史密斯女士:你选择工作时主要考虑什么?

6. 吴先生:我认为工作的性质最重要,千万不要做你没有乐趣的工作。对我而言,愉快的工作环境及有合作精神的同事亦相当重要。

7. 史密斯女士:你认为你将能为这份工作带来什么?

8. 吴先生:我在市场营销方面的工作经验和知识。我对中国市场了解较多,清楚如何开展业务。并且在遇到挑战性的工作时,我是个很努力的人。

Dialogue 4

(Interviewer 面试官:David

Applicant 应聘者:John)

1. David:Good morning, sir. My name is David. I feel honored to have the opportunity to be interviewed.

2. John:Good morning, David. Nice to meet you. I am John. Please give us a brief introduction to yourself.

3. David:OK. I graduated last month and received my bachelor's degree. I majored in business management. My native language is Chinese and I have a good command of English. I can also speak a little French, which I learned in France during my last summer vacation. I think I am a confident, outgoing, enthusiastic, responsible and self-motivated person with a strong sense of cooperation and teamwork.

4. John:OK. Would you please tell me which of these personalities do you think is the most important for this position?

5. David:Confidence is the most important one.

6. John:I agree with you. What work experience do you have?

7. David:I worked as an intern for a small newspaper. My primary responsibility was to sell newspaper advertising to businesses.

8. John:Do you have any questions about our company?

9. David:Could you please tell me something about the job responsibilities?

10. John: Of course. As a salesman for our company, I'm supposed to find new customers and keep in touch with old customers.

11. David:Oh, I see. So I would have the opportunity to generate my own potential customers.

12. John:Certainly. By the way, our office hours are from nine to five, Monday through Friday. I'll call you in a week if you get the job.

13. David:OK. Thank you.

1. 大卫:早上好,我是大卫。很荣幸有这个机会来面试。
2. 约翰:早上好,大卫。很高兴见到你。我是约翰。请你简单做个自我介绍吧。

3. 大卫:好的,我上个月刚毕业并取得了学士学位。主修工商管理,母语为中文,并能熟练掌握英语。上次暑假在法国期间,我也学会了说一些法语。个人认为我是一个自信、随和、乐观、责任心强、积极和有团队精神的人。

4. 约翰:你能说说这个工作最需要什么样的性格吗?

5. 大卫:我认为是自信。

6. 约翰:确实如此。你之前有什么工作经验?

7. 大卫:我以前在一个小报社里做实习生,主要任务是给商家推销报纸广告版面。

8. 约翰:关于公司,你有什么问题要问我的吗?

9. 大卫:能给我介绍下工作职责吗?

10. 约翰:当然可以。作为我们公司的销售人员,我要去开发新的客户并和老客户保持联系。

11. 大卫:我明白了,所以我有机会发展自己的潜在客户。

12. 约翰:当然可以了。顺便说下,我们的工作时间是九点到五点,周一到周五。如果你面试成功,我会一个星期之内打电话给你的。

13. 大卫:好的,谢谢。

Situation 3:About Work Experience 工作经验

(Interviewer 面试官:Mr Smith

Applicant 应聘者:John)

Dialogue 1

1. Mr Smith:Have you got any experience in advertising?

2. John:Yes,I have worked in the Public Relations Department of a company in the past two years and planned the advertising campaigns. Sometimes I have to do the work of a specialist when there's something urgent.

1. 史密斯先生:在广告方面有工作经验吗?

2. 约翰:有。我这两年一直在一家公司的公关部工作。主要负责广告策划。当发生紧急事件时,有时我还需要承担一些专业工作。

Dialogue 2

1. Mr Smith:Do you have any practical experience as a secretary?

2. John: Yes, sir. I acted as a secretary in an insurance company.

3. Mr Smith: Would you tell me the essential qualities a secretary should have?

4. John: Well, to begin with, they need to be diligent, and also, they have to do a lot of things on their own initiative. In addition, they should be able to type, make notes in shorthand, and have skills in report and summary writing, and so on. And most important of all, they should have a better memory than average.

1. 史密斯先生:你有秘书工作的实践经验吗?
2. 约翰:有。我曾在一家保险公司担任秘书一职。
3. 史密斯先生:你能告诉我,作为一名秘书须具备什么样的重要素质?
4. 约翰:嗯,好的。我认为秘书首先应该勤奋;其次,他应该主动做许多事情;最后,他能速记、打字并擅长写报告和工作总结,等等。最重要的是,要比常人有更强的记忆力。

Dialogue 3

1. Mr Smith: What have you learned from jobs you have held?
2. John: Above all, I have learned that what is good for the company is good for me. So I follow my boss's instructions strictly and always keep him or her informed.

1. 史密斯先生:从你以前的工作中你学到了什么?
2. 约翰:我明白做对公司有利的事就是对自己有利,所以我严格遵从指示并经常向我的主管汇报。

Dialogue 4

1. Mr Smith: Do you have any sales experience?
2. John: Yes, I've worked in a fashion shop as salesperson.
3. Mr Smith: Where are you working now?
4. John: I'm working as an export sales representative for a foreign trading company.
5. Mr Smith: How long have you been working there?
6. John: I've been working there since I left my previous employer in 2016.
7. Mr Smith: What were you responsible for at your previous job?
8. John: I was responsible for advertising design.
9. Mr Smith: Well, we'll let you know our decision next week. I hope to give you a

positive reply.

　　10. John: Thank you, that would be great.

　　1. 史密斯先生:你有销售经验吗?
　　2. 约翰:是的,我曾在时装店做过兼职。
　　3. 史密斯先生:现在在哪就职呢?
　　4. 约翰:在一家外贸公司做出口销售。
　　5. 史密斯先生:这份工作已经干了多久?
　　6. 约翰:2016年在上一家公司辞职后就一直做到现在。
　　7. 史密斯先生:那你以前是负责做什么的呢?
　　8. 约翰:广告设计。
　　9. 史密斯先生:我们会在下周给你答复,希望是好消息。
　　10. 约翰:谢谢,那真是太好了。

Situation 4: About Strength & Achievements 优点和成绩

(Interviewer 面试官:Mr Smith
Applicant 应聘者:John)

　　1. Mr Smith: What is your greatest strength?

　　2. John: I think I am very good at planning. I manage my time perfectly so that I can always get things done on time.

　　3. Mr Smith: What are your weak points?

　　4. John: When I think something is right, I will stick to it. Sometimes I might be a little stubborn, but I am now trying to find the right balance between determination and compromise.

　　5. Mr Smith: Do you work well under pressure?

　　6. John: Yes, I find it challenging. However, I believe in planning and proper management of my time to reduce panic deadlines.

　　7. Mr Smith: Are you more of a follower or a leader?

　　8. John: I don't try to go ahead of people and lead them. I'd rather cooperate with everybody else, and get the job done by working together. I don't agree with someone else's opinion if I think they are wrong, but when I understand their thinking and see they

have some good ideas, I'm very happy to go along with them.

9. Mr Smith: How do you deal with those who you think are difficult to deal with?

10. John: I stick to my principles and obey the rules. If they lack enthusiasm, I'll get them involved with something constructive. This often helps them change their attitude later.

11. Mr Smith: Now please tell me something about your achievements in your previous jobs.

12. John: All right, sir. When I was the sales manager of Beijing Friendship Store, I succeeded in raising yearly sales volume by 25% at profit margins from 50% to 80%.

13. Mr Smith: Have you won any rewards?

14. John: Yes. I was chosen as one of "The Big Ten Prominent Youths" of Hubei in 2015.

1. 史密斯先生：你最大的优点是什么？

2. 约翰：我很擅长做计划。我很懂得分配时间，因此总能准时完成任务。

3. 史密斯先生：你的弱点是什么？

4. 约翰：当我认为某事是对的时，我会坚持。有时候，这显得有点顽固，因此我正努力在执着与妥协之间寻求平衡。

5. 史密斯先生：在紧张状态下你能好好工作吗？

6. 约翰：能，我发现那很刺激。但我相信适当地分配时间及周详的计划能减少最后工作期限而带来的恐慌。

7. 史密斯先生：你更像是追随者还是领导者？

8. 约翰：我并不喜欢走在别人前面并领导他们。我更情愿与他人合作，一起把工作做好。当我认为别人观点错误时，我不会赞成。但如果我理解他的想法并发现他有好主意，我会赞同他。

9. 史密斯先生：面对那些你认为难相处的人，你会怎么处理？

10. 约翰：我会坚持自己的原则，并遵守规则。有时，他们只是缺乏工作热情，当我安排他们处理一些建设性的工作时，一些人改变了原来的态度。

11. 史密斯先生：现在请告诉我你的一些工作成果。

12. 约翰：好的，先生。我在北京友谊商店担任销售经理时，成功地把年销售量提到了25%，利润率从50%提到了80%。

13. 史密斯先生：你获得过什么荣誉吗？

14. 约翰:获得过。我曾在2015年被选为湖北"十大杰出青年"。

Situation 5:About Characteristics 谈论性格

(Interviewer 面试官:Mr Smith

Applicant 应聘者:John)

Dialogue 1

1. Mr Smith:What kind of character do you think you have?
2. John:Generally speaking,I am open-minded.
3. Mr Smith:What are your strongest traits?
4. John:Cheerfulness and friendliness.
5. Mr Smith:How would your friends or colleagues describe you?
6. John:They'd say John is friendly,sensitive,caring and determined.
7. Mr Smith:What type of personality do you admire most?
8. John:I admire a person who is honest,flexible and easy-going.
9. Mr Smith:How do you get along with others?
10. John:I get on well with others.

1. 史密斯先生:你认为你是什么性格的人?
2. 约翰:总的来说,我是个思想很开明的人。
3. 史密斯先生:你性格上最大的特点是什么?
4. 约翰:乐观和友好。
5. 史密斯先生:你的朋友或同事怎么形容你?
6. 约翰:他们说约翰是个很友好、敏感、关心他人和有决心的人。
7. 史密斯先生:你欣赏哪种性格的人?
8. 约翰:我欣赏诚实、灵活而且容易相处的人。
9. 史密斯先生:你和别人相处得怎样?
10. 约翰:我和别人相处得很好。

Dialogue 2

1. Mr Smith:What kind of person do you think you are?

2. John: Well, I am always energetic and enthusiastic. They're my strongest characteristics.

3. Mr Smith: What are your strengths and weaknesses?

4. John: Er, as I have said, I'm diligent and industrious. On the other hand, sometimes I'm hardworking and I'm always putting myself under too much pressure to make things perfect.

5. Mr Smith: What qualities would you expect of persons working as a team?

6. John: To work in a team, in my opinion, two characteristics are necessary. He or she must be cooperative and aggressive.

7. Mr Smith: How do you spend your leisure time?

8. John: I like playing games and doing sports. They are my favorite hobbies.

9. Mr Smith: So, what sport do you like most?

10. John: Oh, it's hard to narrow it down to just one. I mean, I like all kinds of sports, basketball, swimming, bike riding and so on. Maybe that's the reason why I am energetic and vigorous.

1. 史密斯先生：你觉得你自己的个性如何？

2. 约翰：嗯，我觉得自己精力很充沛，做事很有热情。这是我最明显的特点了。

3. 史密斯先生：那你认为自己的优点和缺点分别是什么呢？

4. 约翰：正如我刚才说过的，我工作特别勤奋认真。但是，有时为了尽可能把事情办得完美些，我又会让自己背上太多的压力，工作太辛苦。

5. 史密斯先生：你认为作为团队中的一员，一个人需要具备什么样的品质？

6. 约翰：依我之见，作为团队中的一员，合作精神和进取精神两者皆不可少。

7. 史密斯先生：你业余时间都做些什么？

8. 约翰：我爱玩游戏和进行体育运动，这是我最大的爱好。

9. 史密斯先生：那你最喜欢什么体育运动？

10. 约翰：哦，那可实在太多了，我喜欢各类体育运动，打篮球、游泳、骑车之类的。也许这是我精力如此充沛的原因吧。

Ⅸ. Public Security 公共安全篇

The following situational dialogues are about public security which concerns how to report a crime, occupational health, and safety awareness.

以下情景对话是有关公共安全的。对话涉及报案、职业健康以及安全意识等内容。

Situation 1: Reporting a Crime 报案

Dialogue 1

1. Policeman: Hartford Police Station. Can I help you?

2. Susan: I hope so. My house has been burgled.

3. Policeman: Where do you live?

4. Susan: 28 Southbrook Road.

5. Policeman: When did you discover the burglary?

6. Susan: When I got home from work. About 5 minutes ago.

7. Policeman: Was anything stolen?

8. Susan: Yes. All my jewelry's gone, and my computer too. And they sprayed graffiti all over my walls.

9. Policeman: How did they get in?

10. Susan: They forced the back door.

11. Policeman: An officer will be around in about half an hour. Please don't touch anything.

1. 警察：哈特福德警察局，有什么需要帮助吗？

2. 苏珊：希望你们能帮上忙。我家被盗了。

3. 警察：您住在哪？

4. 苏珊：南布鲁克路28号。

5. 警察：您什么时候发现被盗的？

6. 苏珊：大概5分钟前，我下班回家。

7. 警察:丢东西了吗?

8. 苏珊:是的,我所有的首饰都不见了,还有我的电脑也丢了。而且小偷在墙上喷满了涂鸦。

9. 警察:他们是如何进去的?

10. 苏珊:他们从后门破门而入的。

11. 警察:大约半小时后一名警官会到达,请保持现场原样。

Dialogue 2

1. Susan: I'm calling to report a missing credit card.

2. Policeman: What's the card number, miss?

3. Susan: My card number is...

4. Policeman: Was your card lost or stolen?

5. Susan: I left my purse on the counter in the department store while I was in the fitting room to try the dress on.

6. Policeman: When did you discover it was stolen?

7. Susan: I didn't discover that until I went to pay. Someone may be charging things to my account this very minute.

8. Policeman: Once we get your card number, your card will be invalidated all over the world within 30 seconds simply by entering the information into our computer system.

9. Susan: I'm so relieved to hear that.

1. 苏珊:我打电话报警,我的信用卡丢了。

2. 警察:信用卡号码是多少,小姐?

3. 苏珊:我的卡号是……

4. 警察:您的卡是丢失了还是被偷了?

5. 苏珊:我去试衣室试衣时,把钱包放在百货公司的柜台上了。

6. 警察:您什么时候发现信用卡被偷了呢?

7. 苏珊:我去付钱的时候才发现。可能现在就有人正用我的信用卡买东西呢。

8. 警察:我们一弄清您的信用卡号码,只要通知计算机终端,在30秒之内,您的信用卡就会在世界各地失效。

9. 苏珊:你这么说我就放心了。

Situation 2: Health and Safety 健康与安全

Dialogue 1

1. Peter: Sally, will you check these new OH&S posters for me before I put them up?

2. Sally: No problem. You know that I love teamwork!

3. Peter: I think that OH&S is so important that I have made some posters for the office walls to remind people to take a break every hour.

4. Sally: A great idea, Peter. I wish that I had thought of it!

5. Peter: I got the idea because I often get a headache from staring at my computer for too long.

6. Sally: And you think that taking a short break every hour can help?

7. Peter: I know it can. If I get up and have a short break every hour, I feel better and more efficient.

8. Sally: Well, you have taught me something new today. I will try to put your ideas into practice.

9. Peter: We can take a break together and practice English while we relax.

10. Sally: That's the best idea I have heard today!

1. 彼得：莎莉，在我把这些新职业健康和安全海报挂上之前，你能帮我检查一下吗？

2. 莎莉：当然可以，你知道我喜欢团队工作！

3. 彼得：我觉得职业健康和安全太重要了，所以准备了一些海报挂在办公室墙上，提醒大家每隔一小时休息一下。

4. 莎莉：这个主意很好，彼得，真希望是我想到的。

5. 彼得：我想到这个主意是因为我经常因看电脑时间太长而头疼。

6. 莎莉：你认为每小时休息一会儿会有帮助是吗？

7. 彼得：是的。如果每小时站起来休息一会儿，我就会觉得好多了，工作效率也更高。

8. 莎莉：今天你教了我一些新东西。我会试着照你的话去做。

9. 彼得：我们可以一起休息，休息时一起练英语。

10. 莎莉：这是我今天听到的最好的主意！

Dialogue 2

1. Tom: Mum, I'll hang out with my friends.
2. Kate: Okay, who will go with you?
3. Tom: Oh, Mike and Mary.
4. Kate: What are you going to do?
5. Tom: The weather is cold enough, so we've decided to go skating on the lake in Children's Park.
6. Kate: What? Are you crazy?
7. Tom: Come on, mum, take it easy. The ice of the lake is thick enough to hold us.
8. Kate: You silly boy, didn't you watch TV last night?
9. Tom: What do you mean?
10. Kate: The local news said two little kids fell into the lake when they were playing on the lake and lost their lives.
11. Tom: Wow! That was terrible! Really? I didn't realize it was so dangerous.
12. Kate: It sure is. In a mum's eye, a child's safety is the primary concern. Do you understand, dear?
13. Tom: Okay, I'll tell my friends about this and we'll do something else.

1. 汤姆：妈妈，我出去跟朋友玩一会儿。
2. 凯特：好的，和谁一起呢？
3. 汤姆：麦克和玛丽。
4. 凯特：你们想怎么玩？
5. 汤姆：天气很冷，我们决定去儿童公园的湖面上滑冰。
6. 凯特：什么？你们疯了？
7. 汤姆：妈妈，不要紧张啦。湖里的冰够厚啦。
8. 凯特：傻儿子，昨晚没看电视吗？
9. 汤姆：怎么啦？
10. 凯特：本地新闻报道，两个小孩在湖上玩耍时不慎掉进湖里被淹死了。
11. 汤姆：哇！太可怕了！真的吗？我没有意识到这危险。
12. 凯特：当然危险了。在妈妈眼里没有什么比你的安全更重要。亲爱的，知道吗？
13. 汤姆：好的，我会告诉我的朋友们玩点别的。

Part B Group and Team

Test 1

Ⅰ. Presentation(3 minutes)

Suppose you work in the HR Department of a company. Please introduce your company organization to a new staff member based on the following chart.

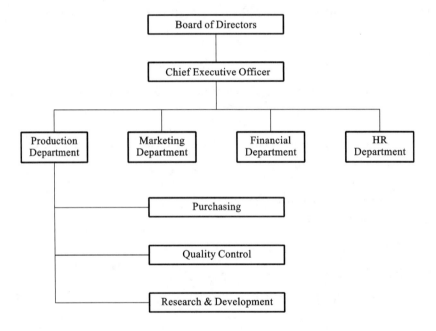

Ⅱ. Interview(3 minutes)

Your department will have a dinner party. Suppose you are making a reservation for the party by telephone. Your conversation should cover the following points.

Q1: At what time can we expect you?

Q2: How many people are there in your party?

Q3: What kind of drink do you need?

Q4: Do you have any special requirements?

- Time: 6 p.m., this Friday evening
- The number of colleagues: 10
- Beverage: beer for male workers and juice for female workers.
- Special requirements: enough meat dishes, cost less than $100, quiet and non-smoking area.

III. Role-play (8 minutes)

Background: Bruce Anderson (CEO of ABC Company) is coming from America to visit your company (TAF). As the sales manager, you (Mathew Lee) are supposed to meet him at the airport and take him to the hotel. The room for Bruce Anderson has been reserved in advance, so you will talk with the receptionist to help him check in. After that, you will show him into Bill Smith's office (your boss).

A: CEO of ABC Company

B: sales manager

C: receptionist

D: boss

IV. PK (5 minutes)

Background: Some young people can't help falling in love with one of his/her colleagues. However, it is clearly specified by some companies that office love is not recommended. What do you think of office love? Choose one side and give your reasons.

Positive side: I'm in favor of office romance.

Negative side: I object to office romance.

Test 2

Ⅰ. Presentation(3 minutes)

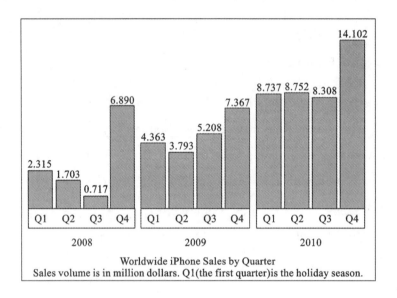

The chart shows the sales of iPhone from 2008 to 2010. You are required to talk about what is shown in it by describing, comparing and summarizing the data. You can add your own comments.

Ⅱ. Interview(3 minutes)

Suppose you are the importer. Please answer the follow questions.

Q1: What's wrong with the goods?

Q2: How do you want to solve the problem?

Q3: I'm sorry for the damage. But it's partially because of the bad weather. Can you accept a 10% discount?

Importer:
- There was a week's delay in delivery.
- About 40% of the goods were damaged.
- The goods were not properly packed.
- Need compensation, replacement of goods or a 30% reduction in price.

Exporter:
- Delay was due to a storm.
- Sorry for the damage.
- Goods were properly packed, but the storm was too violent.
- Admit partial responsibility for the damage.
- Agree to a 10% reduction in price.

III. Role-play(8 minutes)

Background: Four people are discussing whether to launch new products earlier.

Bill Smith(sales manager)　Jenny(assistant to the sales manager):
Sales have been decreasing in the past few months.
Promotional campaigns have been carried out and got a slight increase in sales.
Competitors have launched a series of new products.
Bruce Anderson(manager of Research & Development)　Alex(clerk in R&D):
Slight decrease in sales is not worth the worry.
Testing new products needs enough time.
Launching new products earlier without sound testing is not fair on the customers.
Need more experienced workers.

IV. PK(5 minutes)

Background: Doing one or more part-time jobs seems not fresh at college. What do you think about it? Choose one side and give your reasons.

Positive side: College students should take a part-time job.

Negative side: College students should not take a part-time job.

Test 3

Ⅰ. Presentation(3 minutes)

Task: You are required to give your comments on what people think is the most important about their job.

Ⅱ. Interview(3 minutes)

Now you see a job advertisement.

A Fortune 500 company established in March 1996

World's largest manufacturer, seller of skin care products

Operates in the United States, Canada, Spain, Greece and Russia

Generates nearly $8 billion in annual sales

Join Us!

We're seeking talented candidates

For details please visit

www.rj.com

Task:
- Suppose you are the Human Resources Manager of the company.
- An applicant comes to ask you for information about your company.

Q1: How long is the history of your company?

Q2: What products do you have?

Q3: Do you sell the products at home or abroad?

Q4: How much are your annual sales?

Ⅲ. Role-play(8 minutes)

Background: Job Interview

This company is seeking talented candidates as assistant to the sales manager.

A   John Smith: Director of Human Resources Department

B   Mary: Candidate

C   Henry: Candidate

D   Dick:Candidate

Ⅳ. PK(5 minutes)

Background:More and more young people believe love is based on money. No money, no honey. However,some think true love has nothing to do with money and social status. What do you think of love and money? Choose one side and give your reasons.

Positive side:Love is based on money.

Negative side:Love is not based on money.

Test 4

Ⅰ. Presentation(3 minutes)

Task: You are required to discuss what is shown in the following chart by describing, comparing and summarizing the information. You may add your own comments.

Comparison of income sources between Chinese students and American students.

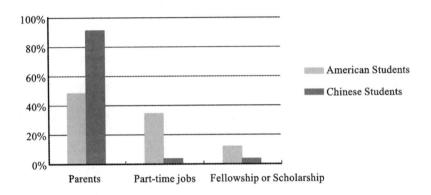

Ⅱ. Interview(3 minutes)

Task: Suppose you work at the Lost and Found Office and your partner, as the owner of the credit card, comes to get his/her credit card back. Ask him/her three questions based on the information provided on the credit card below and your partner should answer the questions.

Q1: By what bank is your card issued?

Q2: What kind of card is it?

Q3: Do you remember your card number?

Q4: Under whose name is the card issued?

Issuer	China Construction Bank
Type	MasterCard, Gold Card(not a Visa Gold Card), UnionPay
Card number	5324580000000087
Name of the card holder	Mr. Yang Ka

III. Role-play(8 minutes)

Background: Li Hong, a clerk in China Bank. Smith, a foreigner from Canada, wants to withdraw a sum of money from an ATM, but he doesn't know how to operate. Now, Li Hong walks towards Smith to help him...

IV. PK(5 minutes)

Background:

The credit card is very useful. It permits people to purchase first and pay later. Therefore, it is helpful to handle some emergencies when the cash is limited. However, it is believed that credit cards may induce people to spend more money. As a result, people may fall into debt. Choose one side and give your reasons.

Positive side: The credit card is very useful.

Negative side: The credit card is not necessary.

Test 5

Ⅰ. Presentation(3 minutes)

Task: Describe the following picture. Explain the phenomenon of "job hopping" in the workplace and analyze some common reasons for people jumping from one job to another.

Ⅱ. Interview(3 minutes)

The following pictures depict a funny job interview. Read the dialogues between the two people and answer the following questions as if you are the interviewee.

Q1: You've had 15 jobs in two months. How can I be sure you are not a job hopper?

Q2: What do you care about most for your workplace?

Q3: What is your ideal boss in your mind?

Ⅲ. Role-play(8 minutes)

The whole family(father, mother and son) were having dinner at a restaurant. They ordered some dishes. After the dishes were served, they were afraid to eat the food. They were thinking about the safety of the food materials.

Task: Make a dialogue of three roles(Father—Jack, Mother—Mary and Son—Tommy) and talk about the food on the dinner table.

IV. PK(5 minutes)

Background: As the economy develops by leaps and bounds, more and more people purchase private cars. Thus our society is witnessing a dramatic growth in the number of private cars. Along with the convenience brought about by private cars, some problems come into being.

Question: Should the use of private cars be limited? Choose one side and give your reasons.

Positive side: The use of private cars should be limited.

Negative side: The use of private cars should not be limited.

Test 6

I. Presentation

You are required to talk about the following illustration for three minutes. Give your account of the elder people driving in the United States and comment on the graph.

II. Interview

Now you will see a copy of a coupon issued by a store. Suppose you are a salesperson and you are supposed to answer questions by a customer about how to use this coupon when making a purchase at the store.

Contestant: A salesperson
Question Master: A customer
No. of Questions: 8-10

Q1: Will I have $25 off if I buy any goods worth $100 or more?

Q2: Can I use the coupon anytime?

Q3: I bought some goods here last week and I still have the receipt now, can you return some cash to me because I have the coupon?

III. Role-play

Suppose you work at a travel agency and you are helping three clients fully understand the travel plan. You will answer questions from the clients.

Tour Dates	Destination	Today's Activities
Day 1	Arrive in Beijing	Airport to hotel transfer(Beijing)
Day 2	Beijing	Tian'anmen Square, The Forbidden City, Treasure Houses, Hutong Tour
Day 3	Beijing	The Temple of Heaven, The Great Wall, Peking Roast Duck
Day 4	Beijing/Xi'an	The Summer Palace, Hotel to airport transfer(Beijing), Airport to hotel transfer(Xi'an)
Day 5	Xi'an	Terracotta Warriors
Day 6	Xi'an/Shanghai	Shanxi History Museum, Hotel to airport transfer(Xi'an), Airport to hotel transfer(Shanghai)
Day 7	Shanghai	Shanghai Urban Planning Exhibition Hall, Shanghai World Financial Center, Yuyuan Market, Yuyuan Garden, The beach of Huangpu River
Day 8	Leave Shanghai	Hotel to airport transfer(Shanghai)

IV. Debate

Would you like to further your education abroad, if it were possible, or just study at home? Give your reasons.

Positive side: College students should further their education abroad to broaden their horizons.

Negative side: It's not necessary for college students to further their education by going abroad.

Test 7

I. Presentation(3 minutes)

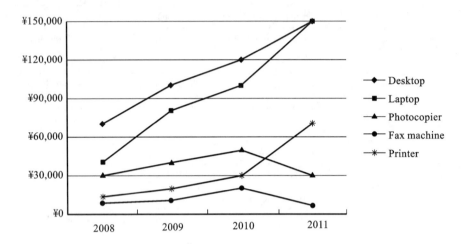

* The line chart above shows the expense on office equipment for PC Electronics in the past four years.

You are required to talk about what is shown in it by describing, comparing and summarizing the data. You can add your own comments.

II. Interview(3 minutes)

Suppose you are working in a restaurant as a waiter or waitress. Now a customer is complaining about food and service. You are going to handle the complaint properly.

Question Master: A customer

Contestant: A waiter or a waitress

Q1: Why is it so hard to get fast service in your restaurant? I've been waiting half an hour!

Q2: Can I see your manager? The fish is not as tender as before.

Q3: The piano really bothers me so much. Can you ask her to stop?

III. Role-play(8 minutes)

Background: The company is having a meeting. Bruce Anderson is chairing the meeting. Alice from Human Resources Department, Mary from the Sales and Marketing Department, and Bill from Customer Service Department, all of the three departments put forward their different issues to be talked about and solved.

A: Bruce Anderson   B: Alice   C: Mary   D: Bill

Ⅳ. PK(5 minutes)

Background: Some people think it is necessary to wear formal clothes in the workplace. But others think it is more comfortable to wear casual clothes. What do you think of the dress code? Choose one side and give your reasons.

Positive side: People should wear formal clothes in the workplace.

Negative side: It's not necessary for people to wear formal clothes at workplace.

Test 8

I. Presentation(3 minutes)

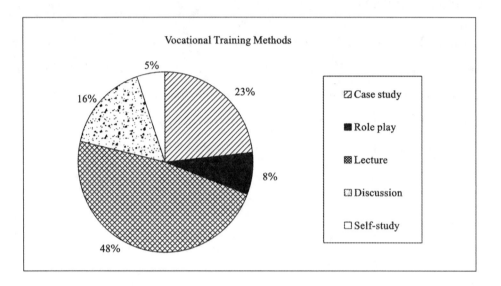

* The pie chart above shows the vocational training methods for new employees of ABC Company. You are required to talk about what is shown in it by describing, comparing and summarizing the data. You can add your own comments.

II. Interview(3 minutes)

Suppose you are having an interview for the position of secretary. You will answer questions from the interviewer.

Contestant: An interviewee

Question Master: An interviewer

Question 1: Can you tell me something about yourself?

Question 2: Why do you want to work here?

Question 3: Why should we hire you?

Question 4: What is your greatest strength?

Question 5: What is your greatest weakness?

Question 6: What relevant experience do you have?

III. Role-play(8 minutes)

Background: Lisa comes to your company to discuss issues about buying the toys your company produces. Bill(CEO of your company)invites Lisa to have a meal and talk business over meal. Mary from the Production Department and Bruce from the Sales and Marketing Department are also joining in the meal.

(It should cover two points: ordering food and discussing business.)

A: Lisa   B: Bill   C: Mary   D: Bruce

IV. PK(5 minutes)

Background: Many people hold "Money is the root of all evil". Other people don't think so. What do you think of money?

Positive side: Money is the root of all evil.

Negative side: Money is not the root of all evil.

Test 9

Ⅰ. Presentation(3 minutes)

Be prepared to talk about the following hotel room rates table, describing, comparing and summarizing the contents. You can also add your own comments.

The room rates of Hongshan Hotel and some of its services

```
                    HONGSHAN HOTEL
                     ROOM RATES
          Suites ------------ $95 per night
         (with bathroom and private sitting room)
          Double room ------------ $65 per night
         (with bathroom and full bar facilities)
          Single room ------------ $50 per night
         (double room, single occupancy rate)
          Economy room ------------ $30 per night
     All rooms are fully equipped with bathrooms and televisions
        Prices include a breakfast served in the coffee shop
         Laundry and business center services are charged
```

Ⅱ. Interview(3 minutes)

Kathy ordered a refrigerator in the store last week, but later found a worrying problem. Now she comes to the store and makes a complaint to the manager, Stefan.

Suppose you are Stefan who is dealing with the complaint.

Q1: Why does this fridge make noises so much?

Q2: I demand you refund me, can you handle it right now?

Q3: Why didn't you check your product before delivery?

Ⅲ. Role-play(8 minutes)

Background: Work in groups to conduct a performance review. Two of you will play the role of the department manager and the HR manager respectively. The rest will play the role of employees in the department. The two managers will listen to each employee's performance report and decide which one performed best last year.

The performance review can be conducted by following the steps below.

Step 1: The HR manager chairs the meeting.
Step 2: The employees report their performance one by one.
Step 3: The managers comment on their performance and decide who performed best last year.
Step 4: The department manager gives his/her expectation for next year.

Ⅳ. PK(5 minutes)

Nowadays, part-time job has become a hot topic in our life, especially among college students. An increasing number of college students have one or even more part-time jobs. Do you think it's good or bad for them?

Side A: It's good for college students to take a part-time job.

Side B: It's bad for college students to take a part-time job.

Test 10

Ⅰ. Presentation(3 minutes)

Here is a cartoon. Please prepare to discuss this picture and students' difficulties in seeking a job.

[word for reference:性别歧视(sex discrimination)]

Ⅱ. Interview(3 minutes)

Suppose you are having an interview for the position of secretary. You will answer questions from the interviewer.

Contestant:An interviewee

Question Master:An interviewer

Question 1:Can you tell me something about yourself?

Question 2:Why do you want to work here?

Question 3:Why should we hire you?

Question 4:What is your greatest strength?

Question 5:What is your greatest weakness?

Question 6:What relevant experience do you have?

Ⅲ. Role-play(8 minutes)

Background:Four people are conducting a job interview. It is supposed that there is a vacant management position in a company. Two members will be interviewees; the other two will be interviewers to decide who will get the job.

IV. PK(5 minutes)

Background: The debates between men and women are never out of date. With the society developing rapidly, the stress caused by it has led to a heated discussion. That is who is more stressed out between men and women.

Positive side: Women are more stressed out than men.

Negative side: Men are more stressed out than women.

Test 11

I. Presentation(3 minutes)

Task: The chart below shows the expenditure on three categories with different proportions among residents in the UK. You are required to talk about the following chart, giving your comments on possible causes of the survey results.

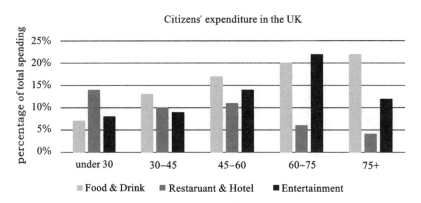

II. Interview(3 minutes)

Suppose you are applying for the salesman position in the Pacific Trading Company. Now you are receiving an interview.

Contestant: Interviewee

Question Master: Interviewer

Questions by the interviewer:

1. Why do you want to apply for this position?
2. Why are you interested in working for our company?
3. Can you tell me your strengths & weaknesses?
4. How many years do you plan to work in this position?
5. What's your working plan in 5 years?
6. Are you a leader or a follower?
7. What have you learned in school?
8. What's your most successful experience?

III. Role-play(8-10 minutes)

Hotel

Task: Suppose two of you want to check in, and the other three are working in the hotel.

Roles for the team members:

Contestant A: Receptionist at the front office

Contestant B: Guest 1 wanting to check in

Contestant C: Guest 2 along with Guest 1 (Guest 1 & Guest 2 are a couple)

Contestant D: Bellboy helping the guests with their luggage and taking them to their room

Contestant E: Room attendant cleaning the room for the guests

IV. PK(5 minutes)

Question: Staying in China, or going abroad for education, which do you think is better?

Positive side: Staying in China for education is better.

Negative side: Going abroad for education is better.

Test 12

Ⅰ. Presentation(3 minutes)

Task: You are required to talk about the following illustration. First, present the information in the illustration and then offer some suggestions about how a business can improve its customer service.

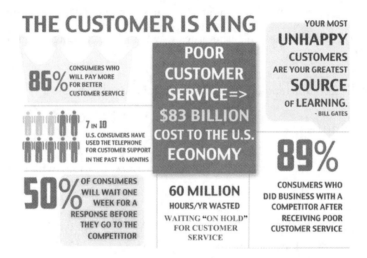

Ⅱ. Interview(3 minutes)

Task: Suppose you're working at People's Trust Insurance Company, and you are talking with a client. You will answer questions from the client.

Contestant: A staff member at People's Trust Insurance Company

Question Master: A client

Question 1: Hello, how quickly can you give me a quote for my homeowners insurance?

Question 2: What is the best price you can quote for my homeowners insurance?

Question 3: What are the various ways I can get a quote for my homeowners insurance?

Question 4: What is the maximum amount you think I might be able to save on my homeowners insurance?

Question 5: How do your insurance plans compare with those of other insurance companies in Florida?

Question 6: Should I worry about your insurance company leaving the state of Florida?

Question 7: Can I customize my policy to my individual needs?

Question 8: What are the qualifications of your agents?

Ⅲ. Role-play(8-10 minutes)

Hospital

Upper left(左上): Tom **Upper right (右上): Jenny**
Lower left(左下): Jack **Lower right (右下): Alice**

Background: Tom is coming to a hospital to see his friend Jenny, who has been ill for some time. But he doesn't know how to get to the in-patient department(住院部). So he asks a man (Jack) for direction at the entrance. Tom goes on according to Jack's direction and runs across(偶遇) Alice who is coming to visit Jenny too. Finally they come to Jenny's ward(病房) together.

Task: Please make a dialogue and role play with your partners.

Ⅳ. PK(5 minutes)

Background: Dancing in public squares is popular across China, but some people complain that the dancing produces too much noise and is a constant irritant to nearby residents. They propose that square dancing should be stopped in public squares.

Question: Should square dancing be stopped in public places?

Positive side: Square dancing should be stopped in public places.

Negative side: Square dancing should not be stopped in public places.

Vocabulary

A

absent   adj. 缺席的;缺少的;心不在焉的;茫然的   vt. 使……缺席

access   n. 进入;使用权;通路

account   n. 账户;解释;账目,账单;理由   vt. 认为;把……视为

achievement   n. 成绩,成就;完成;达到

across   prep. 穿过;横穿   adv. 横过;在对面

action   n. 行动;活动;功能;战斗;情节

actually   adv. 实际上;事实上

adapt   v. 改变以适应环境;改编

admire   vt. 钦佩;赞美

advertising   n. 广告;广告业;登广告   adj. 广告的;广告业的

advocate   n. 提倡者;支持者;律师   vt. 提倡,拥护;为……辩护

affair   n. 事情;事务;私事

afraid   adj. 害怕的;担心的

aggressive   adj. 侵略性的;好斗的;有进取心的

airline   n. 航空公司;航线   adj. 航线的

alcohol   n. 酒精;乙醇

allow   vt. 允许;给予;认可   vi. 容许;考虑

allowance   n. 津贴,零用钱;允许;限额

amazing   adj. 令人惊异的;了不起的

amount   n. 数量;总额

ancient   adj. 古代的;古老的,过时的;年老的   n. 古代人;老人

annual   adj. 年度的;每年的   n. 年刊;年鉴

appetite   n. 食欲;嗜好

applicant   n. 申请人,申请者;请求者

application   n. 应用;申请;应用程序

appointment   n. 任命;约定;任命的职位

appreciate   vt. 欣赏;感激;领会;鉴别   vi. 增值;涨价

area   n. 区域,地区;面积;范围

arrange   vt. 安排;分配

article   n. 文章;物品;条款;[语]冠词   vt. 订约将……收为学徒或见习生;使……受协议条款的约束

artifact   n. 人工制品;手工艺品

assistant   n. 助手;助理;助教   adj. 辅助的,助理的;有帮助的

attractive   adj. 吸引人的;有魅力的;引人注目的

automatic   adj. 自动的;无意识的

autumn   n. 秋天;成熟期;渐衰期,凋落期   adj. 秋天的;秋季的

available   adj. 可获得的;可购得的;可找到的;有空的

Avatar   n. 电影《阿凡达》

avenue   n. 大街;林荫大道;[比喻](达到某目的的)途径,手段,方法,渠道

average   n. 平均;平均数   adj. 平均的;普通的;通常的   vt. 算出……的平均数

award   vt. 授予;判定   n. 奖品;(赔偿)裁定额;(毕业证书等的)授予

awareness   n. 意识,认识;明白,知道

B

bachelor   n. 学士;单身汉

back   n. 后面;背部;靠背;足球等的后卫;书报等的末尾   vt. 支持;后退;背书;下赌注   vi. 后退;背靠;倒退   adv. 以前;向后地;来回地;上溯;回来;回原处   adj. 后面的;过去的;拖欠的

background   n. 背景;隐蔽的位置   vt. 作……的背景   adj. 背景的;发布背景材料的

backpack   n. 双肩背包,背包;远足用的背包   vt. 挑运;把……放入背包   vi. 背负简便行李旅行;挑运

bacon   n. 咸肉;腌肉;熏猪肉

badminton   n. 羽毛球

balance   n. 平衡;余额;匀称   vt. 使……平衡;结算;使……相称

band   n. 带,环;[物]波段;(演奏流行音乐的)乐队;一群   vi. 用带绑扎;给……镶边

bar   n. 条;棒;酒吧;障碍;法庭   vt. 禁止;阻拦   prep. 除……外

basketball   n. 篮球;篮球运动

battery   n. 电池;蓄电池

beefsteak   n. 牛排

beer   n.啤酒   vi.喝啤酒

belt   n.带;腰带;地带   vt.用带子系住;用皮带抽打

benefit   n.利益,好处;救济金   vt.有益于;对……有益

block   n.块;街区;大厦;障碍物   adj.成批的,大块的;交通堵塞的   vt.阻止;阻塞;限制;封盖

borrow   vi.借;借用;从其他语言中引入   vt.借;借用

bouilli   adj.煮过的   n.清煮熟肉

box   n.箱,盒子;包厢;一拳   vi.拳击   vt.拳击;装……入盒中;打耳光

brand   n.商标;牌子

breakfast   n.早餐;早饭   vi.吃早餐   vt.为……供应早餐

breeze   n.微风

briefly   adv.短暂地;简略地;暂时地

bring   vt.带来;促使;引起;使某人处于某种情况或境地

brochure   n.手册;小册子

burgle   vt.偷窃;破门盗窃

burning   adj.燃烧的;强烈的;发热的   n.燃烧

button   n.按钮;纽扣   vt.扣住;扣紧;在……上装纽扣   vi.扣住;装有纽扣;扣上纽扣

C

cabinet   n.橱柜

café   n.[法]咖啡馆

cafeteria   n.(工厂、学校等的)自助餐厅,食堂

camera   n.照相机;摄影机

candidate   n.候选人,候补者;应试者

capital   n.首都,省会;资金;大写字母;资本家   adj.首都的;重要的;大写的

carousel   n.行李传送带

cart   n.推车   vt.用车装载   vi.驾运货马车;用运货车运送

cartoon   n.卡通片,动画片;连环漫画   vt.为……画漫画

catalogue   n.目录

catering   n.承办酒席;提供饮食服务

ceremony   n.仪式;典礼

certainly   adv.当然;行(用于回答);必定

chair   n.椅子;讲座;(会议的)主席位;大学教授的职位   vt.担任(会议的)主席;

使……入座;使就任要职

challenge　n. 挑战;怀疑　vt. 向……挑战;对……质疑

challenging　adj. 挑战性的;引起挑战性兴趣的

change　n. 变化;找回的零钱　vt. 改变;交换　vi. 改变;兑换

character　n. 性格,品质;特性;角色　vt. 印,刻;使具有特征

characteristic　adj. 典型的;特有的;表示特性的　n. 特征;特性;特色

charger　n. 充电器;军马;袭击者;委托者;控诉者

chart　n. 图表;海图;图纸　vt. 绘制……的图表;详细计划

check　vt. 检查,核对;制止,抑制;在……上打钩　vi. 核实,查核;中止;打钩;[象棋]将一军　n. [美]支票;制止,抑制;检验,核对

cheerfulness　n. 高兴;快活

chest　n. 胸,胸部;衣柜;箱子

chop　n. 砍;排骨;商标　vt. 剁碎;砍

cinema　n. 电影;电影院;电影业;电影制作术

claim　n. 要求;声称;索赔;(财产等)所有权　vt. 要求;声称;索赔(钱财)

classical　adj. 古典的;经典的;传统的;第一流的

client　n. [经]客户;顾客;委托人

climate　n. 气候;风气;思潮;风土

coffee　n. 咖啡;咖啡豆;咖啡色

coke　n. 焦炭;可卡因;可口可乐(Coca-Cola)　vi. 焦化　vt. 变成焦炭;用麻药使……麻醉

cola　n. 可乐;可乐树(其籽含咖啡因)

colleague　n. 同事;同僚

college　n. 大学;学院

command　n. 指挥;控制　vt. 命令,指挥;控制;俯瞰

comment　n. 评论;意见;批评　vt. 发表评论;发表意见

compare　n. 比较　vt. 比较;对照;比喻为　vi. 比较;相比

compelling　adj. 引人注目的;强制的;激发兴趣的

competitive　adj. 竞争的,比赛的;(价格等)有竞争力的

complain　vi. 投诉;发牢骚;诉说　vt. 抱怨;控诉

complaint　n. 抱怨;诉苦;疾病;委屈

compromise　n. 妥协,和解;折中方案　vt. 妥协;危害

concert   n. 音乐会；一致；和谐

conduct   n. 行为举止；实施(办法)；引导   vt. 管理；引导；表现

confirmation   n. 确认；证实；证明；批准

connecting flight   转接班机

consecutive   adj. 连贯的；连续不断的

constructive   adj. 建设性的；推定的；构造上的

contestant   n. 竞争者；争辩者

continental   adj. 大陆的；大陆性的   n. 欧洲人

contribute   v. 贡献；捐赠(款项)；投稿(给杂志等)

convenient   adj. 方便的

cooperate   vi. 合作，配合；协力

cooperative   adj. 合作的；合作社的   n. 合作社

cough   n. 咳嗽；咳嗽声   vt. 咳出   vi. 咳嗽

counter   n. 柜台；对立面；计数器   vi. 逆向移动，对着干；反驳   vt. 反击，还击；反向移动，对着干；反驳，回答   adj. 相反的

couple   n. 对；夫妇；数个   vi. 结合；成婚   vt. 结合；连接

course   n. 科目；课程；过程；进程；道路；路线，航向；一道菜

cover   n. 封面，封皮；盖子；掩蔽物；幌子，借口   vt. 包括；采访，报道；涉及

crazy   adj. 疯狂的；狂热的，着迷的

credit   n. 信用；信誉   vt. 相信，信任；把……归于，归功于；赞颂

crime   n. 罪行，犯罪；罪恶；犯罪活动   vt. 控告……违反纪律

croissant   n. 羊角面包；[法]新月形面包

crossing   n. 十字路口；杂交；横渡；横道

crucial   adj. 决定性的；关键性的，极其显要的

culture   n. 文化，文明；修养；栽培   vt. [细胞][微]培养(等于cultivate)

cup   n. 杯子；奖杯；酒杯   vt. 使成杯状；为……拔火罐

currency   n. 货币；通货

customer   n. 顾客；家伙

customize   vt. 定做；按客户具体要求制造

customs   n. 海关；风俗；习惯；关税

cute   adj. 可爱的；漂亮的；聪明的，伶俐的

D

Danish　adj. 丹麦的;丹麦人的;丹麦语(文)的　n. 丹麦语

data　n. 数据(datum 的复数);资料

deadline　n. 截止期限;最后期限

debate　n. 辩论;(正式的)讨论　vt. 辩论;争论;讨论

debit　n. 借方　vt. 记入借方;登入借方

declare　vt. 宣布;声明;断言,宣称

decoration　n. 装饰品;装饰,装潢

definitely　adv. 清楚地,当然,明确地,肯定地

delicate　adj. 微妙的;精美的,雅致的;柔和的;易碎的;纤弱的;清淡可口的

delicious　adj. 美味的;可口的

deliver　vt. 交付;发表;递送

department　n. 部;部门;系;科;局

design　n. 设计;图案　vt. 设计;计划;构思

designer　n. 设计师;设计者;构思者

desire　n. 欲望;要求　vt. 想要;要求;希望得到……

desktop　n. 桌面;台式机

dessert　n. 餐后甜点;甜点心

destination　n. 目的地;终点

determination　n. 决心;果断;测定

diarrhea　n. 腹泻;痢疾

diligent　adj. 勤勉的;用功的,费尽心血的

dining　n. 吃饭;进餐

direct　adj. 直接的

discount　n. 折扣;贴现率　vi. 贴现;打折扣出售商品　vt. 打折扣;将……贴现;贬损;低估;忽视

discover　vt. 发现;发觉

discrimination　n. 歧视;区别;辨别;识别力

dislike　v. 不喜欢;讨厌

display　n. 显示;炫耀　vt. 显示;表现;陈列　adj. 展览的;陈列用的

district　n. 区域;地方

document　n. 文件;公文　vt. 记录;记载

domestic   adj. 国内的;家庭的   n. 国货;用人

dormitory   n. 宿舍;学生宿舍   adj. 住宅区的

dumpling   n. 汤圆;饺子;水果布丁

dust   n. 灰尘;尘埃;尘土   vt. 撒;拂去灰尘   vi. 拂去灰尘;化为粉末

E

economics   n. 经济学;国家的经济状况

economy   n. 经济;节约;理财

edition   n. 版本;版次;集

efficient   adj. 有效率的;有能力的;生效的

electronics   n. 电子学;电子工业

energetic   adj. 精力充沛的;积极的;有力的

engage   vt. 聘用;吸引住   vi. 从事

engineer   n. 工程师;工兵;火车司机   vt. 设计;策划;精明地处理   vi. 设计;建造

enjoy   vt. 欣赏,享受;喜爱;使……过得快活

enjoyable   adj. 快乐的;有乐趣的;令人愉快的

enquiry   n. 询问;盘问

entertainment   n. 娱乐;消遣;款待

enthusiasm   n. 热心;热忱;热情

enthusiastic   adj. 热情的;热心的;狂热的

entrance   n. 入口;进入   vt. 使……出神;使……入迷

escalator   n. 自动扶梯;电动扶梯

essential   adj. 基本的;必要的;本质的;精华的   n. 本质;要素;要点;必需品

establish   vt. 建立;创办;查实,证实

exactly   adv. 恰恰;确切地;精确地

examine   vt. 检查;调查;检测;考试   vi. 检查;调查

exchange   n. 交换;交流;交易所;兑换   vt. 交换;交易;兑换

exhibit   n. 展览品;证据;展示会   vt. 展览;显示;提出(证据等)   vi. 展出;开展览会

exotic   adj. 异国的;外来的;异国情调的

expense   n. 损失,代价;消费   vt. 向……收取费用

experience   n. 经验;经历;体验   vt. 经历;体验

experiment   n. 实验,试验;尝试   vi. 尝试;进行实验

explosive   n. 炸药;爆炸物   adj. 爆炸的;爆炸性的;爆发性的

export   n. 输出,出口;出口商品   vt. 输出;出口

expose   vt. 揭露,揭发;使……曝光;显示

exposition   n. 博览会;展览会

exquisite   adj. 精致的;细腻的;优美的,高雅的;异常的

extend   vt. 延伸;扩大;推广;伸出;给予;对……估价

F

fair   adj. 公平的;美丽的,白皙的;[气象]晴朗的   adv. 公平地;直接地;清楚地   n. 展览会;市集

familiar   adj. 熟悉的;常见的;亲近的   n. 常客;密友

famous   adj. 著名的;极好的,非常令人满意的

fan   n. 迷;风扇;爱好者   vt. 煽动;刺激;吹拂   vi. 成扇形散开;飘动

fancy   adj. 想象的;花哨的

fantastic   adj. 奇异的;空想的;异想天开的;古怪的;极好的,极出色的;不可思议的;不切实际的

fare   n. 票价;费用

fashion   n. 时尚,时装;时装领域,时尚界

favorite   n. 幸运儿;喜欢的事物;收藏夹   adj. 最喜爱的;中意的;宠爱的

fax   n. 传真   vt. 传真

feature   n. 特色;特征   vt. 以……为特色

fee   n. 费用;酬金;小费   vt. 付费给……

fever   n. 发烧;发热   vt. 使发烧;使狂热   vi. 发烧;狂热;患热病

fiction   n. 小说;虚构,编造;谎言

figure   n. 人物;数字;身材   v. 计算

file   n. 文件;档案   vt. 把……归档

fillet   n.（去骨的）肉片;鱼片   v. 剔除(肉或鱼)的骨头

film   n. 电影;薄膜;胶卷;轻烟   vt. 在……上覆以薄膜;把……拍成电影   vi. 摄制电影;生成薄膜;变得朦胧

fine   adj. 好的;优良的;细小的,精美的;健康的;晴朗的   n. 罚款   vt. 罚款;澄清   adv. 很好地;精巧地

firm   adj. 坚定的;牢固的;严格的;结实的   vt. 使……坚定;使……牢固   n. 公司;商号

fit   vt. 安装;使……适应;使……合身;与……相符   vi. 符合,配合;适合;合身

adj. 健康的;合适的;恰当的;准备好的　n. 合身;发作;痉挛

　　flexible　adj. 灵活的;柔韧的;易弯曲的

　　flight　n. 飞行;班机

　　focus　n. 焦点;中心;清晰;焦距　vt. 使……集中;使……聚焦

　　follow　n. 跟随;追随　vi. 跟随;接着　vt. 跟随;遵循;仿效;密切注意,注视;注意;倾听

　　follower　n. 追随者;信徒;属下

　　football　n. 足球;橄榄球

　　force　n. 力量;武力;军队;魄力　vt. 促使,推动;强迫;强加

　　foreign　adj. 外国的;外交的;异质的;不相关的

　　fresh　adj. 新鲜的;清新的;淡水的;无经验的　n. 开始;新生;泛滥

　　fried　adj. 油炸的,油煎的;喝醉了的

　　front　n. 前面;正面;前线　vt. 面对;朝向;对付　vi. 朝向　adj. 前面的;正面的

　　frozen　adj. 冻结的;冷酷的　v. 结冰(freeze 的过去分词)

　　fry　n. 鱼苗;油炸食物　v. 油炸;油煎

G

　　generally　adv. 通常;普遍地,一般地

　　generate　vt. 使……形成;发生;生殖

　　gentlemen　n. 先生;绅士;有教养的人

　　Germany　n. 德国

　　glass　n. 玻璃;玻璃制品;镜子　vt. 用玻璃把(某物)罩住

　　gorgeous　adj. 华丽的;光彩夺目的

　　graduate　vt. 授予……学位;分等级;标上刻度　vi. 毕业;渐变　n. 研究生;毕业生　adj. 毕业的;研究生的

　　graffiti　n. 墙上乱写乱画的东西(graffito 的复数形式)

H

　　hall　n. 过道;会堂;食堂;大厅,前厅

　　ham　n. 火腿;业余无线电爱好者;蹩脚演员　vi. 表演过火　vt. 演得过火

　　hamburger　n. 汉堡包,火腿汉堡;牛肉饼,肉饼;碎牛肉

　　hang　vt. 悬挂,垂下;装饰

　　head　n. 头;上端;最前的部分;理解力　adj. 头的;主要的;在顶端的　vt. 前进;作为……的首领;站在……的前头;给……加标题　vi. 出发;成头状物;船驶往

headache　n. 头痛;麻烦;令人头痛之事

historic　adj. 有历史意义的;历史上著名的

historical　adj. 历史的;史学的;基于史实的

hobby　n. 嗜好;业余爱好

homeowner　n. 私房屋主;自己拥有住房者

honor　n. 荣誉;信用;头衔　vt. 尊敬

horizon　n. 地平线;视野;眼界;范围

host　n. 主人;主办方;东道主　v. 主办

hurry　n. 匆忙,急忙　v. 仓促(做某事);催促;(朝某方向)迅速移动;迅速处理

I

ID　n. 身份证件

illustration　n. 说明;插图;例证;图解

importantly　adv. 重要的是;有名望地;自命不凡地

impractical　adj. 不切实际的;不现实的;无用的

improve　vt. 改善,增进;提高……的价值

include　vt. 包含;包括

incorporation　n. 公司;合并,编入;团体组织

indeed　adv. 甚至;的确,确实

indirect　adj. 间接的

individual　adj. 个人的;个别的;独特的　n. 个人,个体

industrious　adj. 勤勉的

industry　n. 工业;产业;行业

inform　vt. 通知;告诉;报告

initiative　n. 主动权;首创精神　adj. 主动的;自发的;起始的

inn　n. 客栈;旅馆

innovative　adj. 新颖的,创新的

input　n. 投入;输入　vt. [自][电子]输入;将……输入电脑

instruction　n. 指令,命令;指示;教导;用法说明

insurance　n. 保险;保险费;保险契约;赔偿金

interest　n. 兴趣,爱好;利息

intermission　n. 幕间休息;暂停;中断

international　n. 国际体育比赛(选手);外国人　adj. 国际的

interpreter   n. 口译人员

interviewer   n. 采访者;会见者;面谈者;进行面试者

introduce   vt. 介绍;引进;提出;采用

introduction   n. 介绍;引进;采用;入门;传入

invalidate   vt. 使无效;使无价值

item   n. 条款,项目;一则;一件商品(或物品)   v. 记下;逐条列出

itinerary   n. 旅程,路线;旅行日程

J

jacket   n. 短上衣,夹克;文件套,公文夹   vt. 给……穿夹克;给……包上护封

jewelry   n. 珠宝;珠宝类

jog   vt. 慢跑;轻推;蹒跚行进;使颠簸   vi. 慢跑;轻推;蹒跚行进;颠簸着移动   n. 慢跑;轻推,轻撞

join   vt. 参加;结合;连接   vi. 加入;参加;结合   n. 结合;连接;接合点

journal   n. 日报,杂志;日记;分类账

journalist   n. 新闻工作者,新闻记者

juice   n.(水果)汁,液;果汁

K

kid   n. 小孩;小山羊   v. 欺骗;取笑;戏弄   adj. 小山羊皮制的;较年幼的

L

lamb   n. 羔羊,小羊;羔羊肉   v. 生小羊,产羔羊

landmark   n. 地标;里程碑;纪念碑;地界标;划时代的事   adj. 有重大意义或影响的

landscape   n. 风景;风景画;景色;山水画;乡村风景画   vt. 对……做景观美化,给……做园林美化;从事庭园设计

lane   n. 小巷;[航][水运]航线;车道;罚球区

language   n. 语言;语言文字;表达能力

languid   adj. 倦怠的;懒洋洋的

laptop   n. 笔记本电脑

large   adj. 大的;多数的;广博的

lasting   adj. 持久的;永恒的   v. 持续;维持(last 的-ing 形式)

layover   n. 中途短暂的停留 (尤指长途飞行的)

leave   vt. 离开;留下;遗忘;委托   vi. 离开;出发;留下   n. 许可,同意;休假

leisure   n. 闲暇;空闲;安逸   adj. 空闲的;有闲的;业余的

librarian　n.图书馆员;图书管理员

library　n.图书馆,藏书室;文库

light　n.光,光线;灯　adj.轻的;浅色的;明亮的;轻松的;容易的;清淡的　vt.照亮;点燃

literature　n.文学;文献;文艺;著作

local　adj.当地的;局部的;地方性的;乡土的

low-carbon　adj.低碳的,含碳量低的

luggage　n.行李;皮箱

lullaby　n.摇篮曲;催眠曲

lung　n.肺;呼吸器

M

magazine　n.杂志;弹药库;胶卷盒

magnificent　adj.高尚的;壮丽的;华丽的;宏伟的

major　adj.主要的;重要的;主修的;较多的　n.[人类]成年人;主修科目;陆军少校　vi.主修

margin　n.边缘;利润,余裕;页边的空白　vt.加边于;加旁注于

marketing　n.促销,销售;市场营销

mascot　n.吉祥物

match　vt.使……相配

maximum　n.[数]极大,最大限度;最大量　adj.最高的;最多的;最大极限的

may　aux.可能,也许;能够;祝愿　n.五月

medium　adj.中间的,中等的;半生熟的　n.方法;媒体;媒介;中间物

memory　n.记忆,记忆力;内存,[计]存储器;回忆

menu　n.菜单

middle　adj.中间的,中部的;中级的,中等的　n.中间,中央;腰部

mind　n.理智,精神;意见;智力;记忆力　vt.介意;专心于;照料　vi.介意;注意

minute　n.分,分钟;片刻,一会儿;备忘录,笔记;会议记录　vt.将……记录下来　adj.微小的;详细的

misplace　vt.放错地方;忘记把……放在什么地方;错误地信任某人

model　n.模型;模式;模特　vt.模仿;制作模型,塑造

moment　n.片刻;瞬间;时刻;重要,契机

motivated　adj.有动机的;有积极性的

mouth n. 口,嘴;河口 vt. 做作地说,装腔作势地说;喃喃地说出 vi. 装腔作势说话

movie n. 电影;电影院;电影业 adj. 电影的

N

narrow adj. 狭窄的,有限的;勉强的;精密的;度量小的 n. 海峡;狭窄部分,隘路 vt. 使……变狭窄

near adj. 近的;近亲的;近似的 adv. 近;接近 prep. 靠近;近似于

necessarily adv. 必要地;必定地;必然地

nervous adj. 神经的;紧张不安的

non-stop adj. 直达的;不休息的 adv. 不休息地

novel adj. 新奇的;异常的 n. 小说

O

objective adj. 客观的;目标的;宾格的 n. 目的;目标

occupational adj. 职业的;占领的

offer vt. 提供;出价;试图 vi. 提议;出现;献祭;求婚 n. 提议;出价;意图;录取通知书

operate vt. 操作;经营

opportunity n. 时机;机会

orange adj. 橙色的;橘色的 n. 橙色;橙树,橘树

order n. 命令;顺序;规则;[贸易]订单 vt. 命令;整理;订购 vi. 命令;订货

outgoing adj. 对人友好的,开朗的;外出的 n. 外出 v. 超过;优于

outstanding adj. 杰出的;显著的;未解决的;未偿付的 n. 未偿贷款

P

package n. 包,包裹;套装;套餐

pancake n. 薄烤饼;粉饼

panic n. 恐慌,惊慌;大恐慌 adj. 恐慌的;没有理由的 vt. 使恐慌

party n. 政党,党派;聚会,派对;当事人

pass n. 及格;经过;护照;途径;传球 v. 经过;传递;变化;终止

passport n. 护照;通行证

password n. 密码;口令

pastry n. 油酥点心;面粉糕饼

pavilion n. 阁;亭子;大帐篷;展馆 vt. 搭帐篷;置……于亭中;笼罩

pay vt. 支付,付;偿还,补偿;给予 vi. 付款;偿还 n. 工资,薪水;付款;报答

peace   n. 和平;平静;和睦;秩序

perform   vt. 执行;完成;演奏   vi. 执行,机器运转;表演

perfume   n. 香水;香味   vt. 洒香水于……;使……带香味   vi. 散发香气

personal   adj. 个人的;身体的;亲自的   n. 人事消息栏

personality   n. 个性;品格;名人

personnel   n. 人员;人事;全体员工

photocopier   n. 影印机;复印机

photographer   n. 摄影师;照相师

photography   n. 摄影;摄影术

pizza   n. 比萨饼(一种涂有乳酪和番茄酱的意大利式有馅烘饼)

plant   n. 工厂,车间;植物;设备;庄稼   vt. 种植;培养;栽培;安置

playground   n. 运动场,操场;游乐场

politics   n. 政治,政治学;政治活动;政纲

poolside   adj. 在游泳池边的   n. 游泳池边

popcorn   n. 爆米花,爆玉米花

pork   n. 猪肉

portable   n. 手提式打字机   adj. 手提的,便携式的;轻便的

position   n. 位置,方位;职位,工作;姿态;站位   vt. 安置;把……放在适当位置

poster   n. 海报,广告;招贴

potential   n. 潜能;可能性   adj. 潜在的;可能的;势的

practice   n. 实践;练习;惯例   v. 练习;实习;实行

precious   adj. 宝贵的;珍贵的;矫揉造作的

prefer   vt. 更喜欢;宁愿;提出;提升   vi. 喜欢;愿意

prepare   vt. 准备;使……适合;装备;起草

present   vt. 提出;介绍;呈现;赠送   adj. 现在的;出席的

presentation   n. 描述,陈述;介绍;赠送

press   vt. 压;按;逼迫;紧抱   vi. 压;逼;重压   n. 压;按;新闻;出版社;[印刷]印刷机

pressure   n. 压力;压迫,[物]压强   vt. 迫使;密封;使……增压

previous   adj. 以前的;早先的

primary   adj. 主要的;初级的;基本的

printer   n. [计]打印机;印刷工;印花工

probably   adv. 大概;或许;很可能

profession　n. 职业；专业

professional　adj. 专业的；职业的；职业性的　n. 专业人员；职业运动员

profit　n. 利润；利益　vt. 有益于

prohibit　vt. 阻止；禁止

prominent　adj. 突出的，显著的；杰出的，卓越的

proper　adj. 适当的；本身的；特有的；正派的　adv. 完全地

properly　adv. 适当地；正确地；恰当地

protection　n. 保护；防卫

province　n. 省；领域；职权

publish　vt. 出版；发表；公布

punch　n. 冲压机；打洞器；钻孔机　vt. 开洞；以拳重击　vi. 用拳猛击

purse　n.（女士）手提袋　vt.（嘴巴）皱起，使……缩拢；噘嘴

Q

qualify　vt. 限制；使具有资格；证明……合格

quick　adj. 快的；敏捷的；灵敏的　adv. 迅速地；敏捷地

quote　vt. 报价；引述；举例说明

R

rapidly　adv. 迅速地；很快地；立即

rate　vt. 认为；估价

reasonable　adj. 合理的，公道的；明白道理的；有理性的

receipt　n. 收到；收据；收入　vt. 收到

recently　adv. 最近；新近

reclaim　n. 改造，感化；再生胶　vt. 开拓；回收再利用；改造某人，使某人悔改　vi. 抗议，喊叫

recommend　vt. 推荐，介绍；劝告；使受欢迎；托付　vi. 推荐；建议

register　vt. 登记；注册

relaxing　adj. 令人轻松的

relevant　adj. 相关的；切题的；中肯的；有重大关系的

relieve　vt. 解除；减轻

remind　vt. 提醒；使……想起

remittance　n. 汇款；汇寄之款；汇款额

renew　vt. 使……更新；续借；续费；复兴；重申　vi. 更新；重新开始

representative　adj. 典型的,有代表性的;代议制的　n. 代表;典型;众议员

reputation　n. 名声,名誉;声望

require　vt. 需要;要求;命令

reservation　n. 预约,预订;保留

reserve　n. 储备,储存;自然保护区;预备队;缄默;[金融]储备金　vt. 储备;保留;预约

resort　n. 凭借,手段;度假胜地;常去之地　vi. 求助,诉诸;常去;采取某手段或方法

resource　n. 资源,财力;办法;智谋

restaurant　n. 餐馆;饭店

return　v. 返回;报答　n. 返回;归还;回球　adj. 报答的;回程的;返回的

rewarding　adj. 有益的,值得的;有报酬的,报答的

ride　vi. 骑马;乘车;依靠;飘浮　vt. 骑;乘;控制;(骑马、自行车等)穿越;搭乘;飘浮　n. 骑;乘坐;(骑马、自行车等的)旅行;旅程

right　adj. 正确的;直接的;右方的　vt. 纠正　vi. 复正;恢复平稳　n. 正确;右边;正义;权利　adv. 正确地;恰当地;彻底地

roast　vt. 烤,焙;烘,烘烤;(使)受热发烫　vi. 烤;烘　adj. 烘烤的;(食物)烤过的　n. 烤肉;烘烤

roll　vt. 卷;滚动,转动;辗　vi. 卷;滚动;转动;起伏,摇晃　n. 卷;卷形物;名单;摇晃

romance　n. 传奇;浪漫史;风流韵事;冒险故事　vi. 虚构;渲染;写传奇

run　vi. 经营;奔跑;运转　vt. 管理,经营;运行;参赛　n. 奔跑;赛跑;趋向;奔跑的路程

rush　n. 冲进;仓促;急流;忙乱　adj. 急需的　vt. 突袭;匆忙地做;飞跃　vi. 冲;奔;闯;赶紧;涌现

S

sale　n. 销售;出售;拍卖;销售额;廉价出售

sales　n. 销售(sale 的复数);销售额

sample　n. 样品;样本;例子

sausage　n. 香肠;腊肠;装香肠的碎肉

scale　n. 规模;比例;鳞;刻度;天平;数值范围　vt. 测量;攀登;刮鳞;依比例决定　vi. 衡量;攀登;剥落;生水垢

schedule　vt. 安排,计划;编制目录;将……列入计划表　n. 时间表;计划表;一览表

science　n. 科学;技术;学科;理科

seaside　n. 海边;海滨　adj. 海边的;海滨的

seat　n. 座位;所在地;职位　vt. 使……坐下;可容纳……的;使就职

secretary　n. 秘书;书记;部长;大臣

security　n. 安全;保证;证券;抵押品　adj. 安全的;保安的;保密的

semester　n. 学期;半年

sensitive　adj. 敏感的;感觉的;易受伤害的;易受影响的　n. 敏感的人;有灵异能力的人

shirt　n. 衬衫;汗衫,内衣

shorthand　n. 速记;速记法　adj. 速记法的

sightseeing　n. 观光;游览　adj. 观光的;游览的

sign　n. 迹象;符号;记号;手势;指示牌　vi. 签署;签名　vt. 签署;示意

sit　vi. 坐;位于　vt. 使……就座

situational　adj. 环境形成的;情形的

sleeper　n. 卧车;卧铺;枕木;沉睡者

snack　n. 小吃,快餐;易办到的事,小事一桩　vi. 吃快餐,吃点心

sound　vt. 听(诊);测量,测……深;使发声;试探;宣告　vi. 听起来;发出声音;回响;测深　n. 声音,语音;噪音;海峡;吵闹;听力范围　adj. 健全的,健康的;合理的;可靠的;彻底的　adv. 彻底地,充分地

soup　n. 汤,羹;马力　vt. 加速;增加马力

sour　adj. 酸的;发酵的;刺耳的;酸臭的;讨厌的　vi. 发酵;变酸;厌烦　vt. 使变酸;使失望　n. 酸味;苦差事

southern　adj. 南的;南方的　n. 南方人

spaghetti　n. 意大利式细面条

special　adj. 特别的;专门的

specialty　n. 专业,专长;特产;特性;招牌菜　adj. 特色的;专门的;独立的

spray　n. 喷雾;喷雾器;水沫

stare　vt. 凝视,盯着看

start　vt. 开始;启动　vi. 出发　n. 开始;起点

stolen　adj. 偷走的

stranger　n. 陌生人;外地人;局外人

street　n. 街道

strength　n. 力量;力气;兵力;长处

stress　n. 压力;强调;紧张;重要性;重读　vt. 强调;使紧张;加压力于;用重音读

strictly　adv. 严格地;完全地;确实地

structure   n.结构;构造;建筑物   vt.组织;构成;建造

stubborn   adj.顽固的;顽强的;难处理的

subway   n.地铁;地道   vi.乘地铁

succeed   vi.成功;继承;继任;兴旺   vt.继承;接替;继……之后

suggest   vt.提议,建议;启发;使人想起;显示;暗示

suitcase   n.手提箱;衣箱

summarize   vt.总结;概述   vi.做总结;做概括

summary   adj.简易的;扼要的   n.概要;摘要;总结

sunbathing   n.日光浴

suppose   vt.假设;认为;让(虚拟语气);推想   vi.猜想;料想   conj.假使……结果会怎样

suspense   n.悬念;悬疑;焦虑;悬而不决

sweaty   adj.出汗的;吃力的;使人出汗的

symbolize   vt.象征;用符号表现   vi.采用象征;使用符号;作为……的象征

symphony   n.交响乐;谐声,和声

T

table   n.桌子;表格;平地层   vt.制表;搁置;嵌合

tackle   vt.处理

tart   adj.酸的;锋利的;尖刻的   n.果馅饼   vt.打扮

technology   n.科技(总称);工业技术

temporarily   adv.临时地

tennis   n.网球(运动)

term   n.术语;学期;期限;条款

terminal   n.末端;终点;终端机   adj.末端的;终点的;晚期的

terrible   adj.可怕的;很糟的;令人讨厌的   adv.很,非常

thick   n.最拥挤部分   adj.厚的;浓的;粗壮的

ticket   n.票;入场券,标签;(美)候选人名单;证明书;交通罚款单   vt.加标签于;指派;对……开出交通违规罚单

tired   adj.疲倦的;厌倦的,厌烦的

toast   n.干杯;烤面包;接受敬酒的人;(在某领域)广受赞誉的人   vt.向……祝酒,为……干杯   vi.烤火,取暖;使暖和;烘烤(面包片等)

tobacco   n.烟草,烟叶;烟草制品;抽烟

toilet　n. 厕所;盥洗室

toiletries　n. 化妆品;化妆用具;旅行洗漱包

tomato　n. 番茄;西红柿

touch　vt. 接触;触动;给(某人)造成伤害

tower　n. 塔;高楼;堡垒　vi. 高耸;超越

trait　n. 特性,特点;品质;少许

transaction　n. 交易;事务;办理

transfer　n. 转让;转移;传递;(工作的)调动;(财产的)转让　vt. 使转移;调任　vi. 转让;转学;换乘

tripod　n. [摄]三脚架;三脚桌

Tsingtao　n. 青岛(山东省的一个港口城市)

type　n. 类型,品种;模范;样式　vt. 打字;测定(血等)类型　vi. 打字

typical　adj. 典型的;特有的;象征性的

U

urgent　adj. 紧急的;急迫的

V

vacant　adj. 空虚的;空的;空缺的;空闲的;茫然的

vacuum　n. 真空;空间;真空吸尘器　adj. 真空的,利用真空的;产生真空的　vt. 用真空吸尘器清扫

various　adj. 各种各样的;多方面的

vase　n. 瓶;花瓶

view　n. 观察;视野;意见;风景　vt. 观察;考虑;查看

vigorous　adj. 有力的;精力充沛的

violin　n. 小提琴;小提琴手

visa　n. 签证　vt. 签发签证

volleyball　n. 排球

volume　n. 量;体积;卷;音量;大量;册　adj. 大量的

W

waiter　n. 服务员;侍者

wallet　n. 钱包;皮夹

water　n. 水;海水;雨水;海域,大片的水　vt. 供以水;给……浇水　vi. 加水;流泪;流口水

weather   n. 天气;气象;气候;处境   vt. 经受住;使风化;侵蚀;使受风吹雨打   adj. 露天的;迎风的

welfare   n. 福利;幸福;福利事业;安宁   adj. 福利的

well-done   adj. 干得好的;完全煮熟的   int. 好;干得好

western   adj. 西方的,西部的;有西方特征的

window   n. 窗;窗口;窗户

withdraw   vt. 撤退;收回;(从银行)取钱

withdrawal   n. 撤退,收回;提款;取消;退股

wonder   n. 惊奇;奇迹;有特效的东西   v. 想知道;(用于询问时)不知道;感到疑惑;感到惊叹   adj. 奇妙的;非凡的

wool   n. 羊毛;毛线;绒线;毛织品;毛料衣物

woolen   adj. 羊毛的;羊毛制的

workmanship   n. 手艺,工艺;技巧

worm   n. 虫;蠕虫

worthwhile   adj. 值得做的;值得花时间的

X

X-ray   n. 射线;射线照片   adj. X 线的   vt. 用 X 线检查